Genes Don't Lie

DNA

Zetta Thomelin

Grosvenor House
Publishing Limited

All rights reserved
Copyright © Zetta Thomelin, 2025

The right of Zetta Thomelin to be identified as the author of this work has been asserted in accordance with Section 78 of the Copyright, Designs and Patents Act 1988

The book cover is copyright to Zetta Thomelin

This book is published by
Grosvenor House Publishing Ltd
Link House
140 The Broadway, Tolworth, Surrey, KT6 7HT.
www.grosvenorhousepublishing.co.uk

This book is sold subject to the conditions that it shall not, by way of trade or otherwise, be lent, resold, hired out or otherwise circulated without the author's or publisher's prior consent in any form of binding or cover other than that in which it is published and without a similar condition including this condition being imposed on the subsequent purchaser.

A CIP record for this book
is available from the British Library

Paperback ISBN 978-1-83615-246-0
Hardback ISBN 978-1-83615-247-7
eBook ISBN 978-1-83615-248-4

The moral rights of the author have been asserted.

For my sister and for Evi

Also by Zetta Thomelin

Books

The Healing Metaphor – Hypnotherapy Scripts
Self-Help? Self-Hypnosis!
The Trauma Effect – Healing and resolving inherited trauma

Audio

Journeys into Nature
Avebury and Silbury Hill
Sleep
Journey into Sleep
Relieve Stress
Managing Anxiety

Contents

INTRODUCTION	1
Part One – My Story	**5**
Chapter one THE BEGINNING	7
Chapter two THE TEST	18
Chapter three MEETING MY SISTER	24
Chapter four VISITING GRAVES	31
Chapter five A NEW FAMILY	41
Part Two – The Therapy Part	**47**
HOW TO USE THIS SECTION	48
Chapter six IDENTITY	49
Chapter seven SECRETS AND LIES	77
Chapter eight EMOTIONAL STATES – BLAME	87
Chapter nine EMOTIONAL STATES – SHAME	92
Chapter ten EMOTIONAL STATES – GRIEF AND LOSS	101
Chapter eleven EMOTIONAL STATES – ANGER	115
Chapter twelve EMOTIONAL STATES – BELONGING	125
Chapter thirteen INTEGRATING THE PAST – MEETING IN THE SUBCONSCIOUS	133

Chapter fourteen FAMILY CONSTELLATION
OR SYSTEMIC THERAPY   145
Chapter fifteen CONCLUSION   164

ACKNOWLEDGEMENTS   167
REFERENCES   170

INTRODUCTION

Genes don't lie, but people do!

With the cheap and easy access to DNA testing now available, more and more people are discovering they are not who they thought they were or that the make-up of their family has changed. It may have happened to you, and you want to know how to process it. It may have happened to a friend or family member, and you want to help them. I want to create a resource to help others facing such challenges to the sense of self that this brings.

It is not a new experience. In the past, finding out you were adopted would have brought the same challenges. It is now happening, though, on a larger scale. The genie is out of the bottle, and many do not know what to do next.

I had just finished writing my book, *The Trauma Effect*, about inherited trauma, where I shone a light upon a trauma in my family and examined how this impacted me when a new family story surfaced. I had made my peace with my family past at last, and then I found that my family story was an illusion.

An email popped into my inbox which changed everything. Yet another new family secret, about which I had no inkling, was now bobbing up into the light and I had to deal with it.

Every other book I pick up or TV drama I watch has the twist in the tail of someone discovering through

DNA that they were not who they thought they were. With the increasing number of people interested in their ancestry, this can only continue to grow.

I was not the one most affected by my DNA test results; I was still my father's child, but I discovered I had a half-sister, and it was so hard to know how to support her whilst trying to deal with my own changing landscape.

My story is far from unique. It is a story told up and down the land, but little is written to help with processing the story, the complete reframing of all you believed about your family and who you are. It was hardest, of course, for my sister, who said to me only the other day, 'Nobody is talking about how it feels to be me, to find out I am someone other than who I thought I was'.

As I find it so therapeutic to write, I decided to write our story, our feelings, our journey, in the hope that if you share this story, you might feel less alone, and it may help your healing. If no such drama has touched your family, then maybe hearing of ours may help you to value your own story.

When I began to write, it automatically fell into the style of discourse with my father at first, a father who had become a stranger to me now. He was not the man I had loved, and I needed to get to know him again. I needed the opportunity to tell him how I felt and, if she would allow it, a little of how my sister felt. Then I could begin to understand it more. As I wrote the first section, it read rather like a novel, and I hoped this would engage the reader to follow the journey towards understanding.

The therapeutic part naturally followed as I delved deeper and deeper into the feelings of everyone concerned. I wanted to understand the emotions involved in such an experience and, very importantly, what identity means to us, as I think it is the challenge to identity that raises so much emotion. As I am a therapist, I then wanted to come up with a plan to help, presenting ideas that I have used with others on a similar path.

If such a thing has not happened in your world, some of the ideas here may still resonate, such as that of identity, loss and family constellations. So here is our story and journey towards healing. I hope that it can help your healing too.

Zetta Thomelin

Part One – My Story

Chapter one

THE BEGINNING

I know about it now and there is no unknowing for any of us. I had a trigger that set my fingers tapping across the keys. It is my first time in France (the land my father loved so much) since I found out about it. My partner and I are in Paris, a city we had enjoyed separately and now want to share with each other.

Paris, the city of romance. The French, the lovers of Europe. Beauty surrounds us in the architecture, the clothes, the smells that escape the cafes and restaurants, and the sounds that pulse out of the organ at L'eglise de St-Pierre; we are entranced. There is the hustle and bustle of the streets of Montmartre, vendors touting their wares. We smile as we wander and wonder, hand in hand.

But beneath the veneer of the city are the cracks, the imperfections, and the slight smell of urine wafting up from the warming streets. The beggar with plastic bags upon his feet for shoes. The stark metaphor in Gare de Lyon, as we search for a map we can take away, to find only a vending machine for condoms, speaks boldly of the reality beneath the charm of the city, a metaphor of the city; maybe there is another metaphor there too.

I see beneath the intellect, the beauty and charm to the cracks beneath, the feet of clay, and relate it to my father, the man within.

We expect too much from the city of lovers; perhaps I expected too much of my father. I loved him too much, and now he has let me down and is not here to face the music, to see the damage he left behind him.

I cannot help but think of him here. When he was alive and I arrived in France, I would always phone and say, '*Je suis arrivé en France, Papa*', and I would even hear his smile down the line. It is even more present here in Paris, the thought of him, the place he went from boy to man, a place he knew so well, and I want to talk to him, to shout at him. I want answers from him as I go over and over in my mind the stories he used to tell of that French side of his life, mining for clues, looking for signs of the man I did not know but thought I had.

Of course, you know Paris well, Dad. That was where you did your military service, at Le Bourget, the *l'armee de l'air*, following in your father's footsteps – and such footsteps they were.

I remember the stories you told me as I wander these streets. You explained why you were here. You could have done your military service in England or in France. As you were a French national, you made an active choice to do it in France, but they did their military service at 21 and you were all of 18.

I remember you telling me how the other men teased you when you arrived because of the copious, nay, voluminous underwear that your mother had sent with your kit to make sure your private parts were kept safe from pressure. The men in your hut were tough lads, older than you, wise to the ways of the world. What a boy you must have seemed to them.

You said that rules in France are made to be broken. That triggers some thoughts now. You told me how you climbed over the wall to get off the air base to enjoy the delights of Paris. Did it begin then, I wonder? This young man away from home for the first time, handsome in his uniform, did you discover how women were drawn to you then? How easy it was for you? Too easy, perhaps. I had not thought of it before, so young and with Paris at your feet.

There was that night when you were caught on your way back to the base by an officer when you should not have been out. He piled you and your friends into the back of his car and smuggled you back onto the base. Now that would never happen in England. You would be on short rations for weeks.

Speaking of rations, you told me about the red wine served with all your meals and how one day, you were asked to put a tube into a keg and suck the wine up to the surface as the level had dropped very low. You did not lower the tube far enough and just sucked and sucked at the wine fumes. Ten minutes later, you were found unconscious, lying flat on your back on the floor; this young man without a head for wine, well, not yet! Such a funny image I see in my mind's eye, with the older lads laughing and pointing, standing around your prone form.

My favourite story of those days was that one when you were on guard duty at the perimeter of the base, standing tall, standing proud in your uniform, clutching your rifle in your hands, and two men wandered towards you in blue workman's overalls, berets, a cigarette somehow clutched at the edge of the lips as they talked. They slouched along towards you and you lifted your rifle. Your moment had come. '*Arrêter qui y va,*' you shouted. They did not even look over but carried on with that shambling gait, moving nearer. '*Aarrêter qui y va*', you try again, and one of the men glanced towards you as he passed. '*Bon soir garçon*', he said and they moved on by. Your cheeks were flushed. Embarrassed, you peered around to see if anybody had seen. Nobody, thank goodness. So you watched them amble away and resumed your dutiful, erect, proud stance, your rifle at your shoulder!

I love the thought of the picture of you in your uniform, so fresh-faced, boyish, with that cheeky half smile facing the camera. No wonder those men did not take you seriously.

Of course, it was not all funny stories, was it?

No. I also remember how you sounded. Still it caught in your throat when you told me about being part of the guard of honour as they flew in the dead bodies of soldiers being repatriated to France from the troubles in Algiers. It could have been you. You knew this as you stood trying to look straight ahead, trying to mask the emotion you felt, watching other boys' bodies being flown in, other mothers' sons, and it troubled you. You trembled a little, but you stood firm as they passed along the line of men. Did they play 'La Marseillaise', I wonder?

You wrote to your father and told him you did not think you could stick it out. He kindly but firmly told you that you had to do your duty as he had done his.

He had been a pilot in the First World War, winning the Croix de Guerre six times and finally being awarded the *Legion D'honneur*. You did not know how to live up to that, did you? Known in the Air Force as the son of a great man, inside, you trembled at the thought of the dead boys coming home.

Time to toughen up or find a way to ease the pain. Maybe that was it, how life-affirming passion can be in the face of death. Maybe it would be your turn next to be sent to fight and to die, so blot it out, find a way.

She emailed me today, Dad. It was such a surprise. I thought it would have to be me, but she did it, she wants us to meet. It still feels so strange, as if I have just taken a wrong turn and stepped into someone else's story.

I am wondering if it would be easier if it were someone I had never heard of. Do you think? I would have no preconceptions; the sheet would be blank. Or maybe, just maybe, then it would be easier to walk away, refuse to step into this new story – the story you wrote for me without telling me – and exit stage right before the lights went down, leaving me to ad-lib my way through.

Can we build something so late? I mean, I am 57 now, what do you think?

Did I know you at all, Dad? Did you know about this and keep it from us both all these years? That is what plagues me, the fact that I will never know. I will never know if you kept this huge thing from me, even as I sat with you dying, holding your hand, not a blink, not a stutter, no last-minute confessions, well, not to me.

I wonder, now, what that priest heard on the stifling June day as he anointed you with holy oil so you could pass on trouble-free.

I am having to remake you in my mind, Dad. You have become a stranger.

Is everything I knew about you going to be changed, tarnished in some way?

It feels like how it would feel to find out your partner has been unfaithful to you; they are not who you thought them to be anymore. But you are my dad, not my partner. Why do I feel you have betrayed me, been unfaithful to me?

It makes me think about some of your attitudes and the stories you told in a new light. I should have considered it before. Why had I not considered it before?

You talked about all the high-class prostitutes that used to bank at the Credit Lyonnais when you worked there.

I remember you describing their clothes and how charming they were. There was no censure in your tone; if anything, admiration. I am now considering, Dad, whether this is a normal thing to discuss with your daughter.

Of course, I do not expect you to be critical of women who have chosen this path, perhaps their only path to earn a living. I am now, in retrospect, a little shocked at your having this discussion with me, your daughter. Dare I even risk wondering if you knew some of these women rather too well?

Your liberal attitudes to sex were, of course, helpful to me. I remember when I was fourteen, and you told me that if I wanted to have sex, you would rather I did it under your roof than on a park bench somewhere. I was a little stunned, as at that age, I was not ready to embark on such intimacy. But when the time came, I was always bragging to my friends about how liberal things were at home, and that suited me fine.

Everything has a price tag, doesn't it? This gave you free rein, too. At least I could never call you a hypocrite, Dad. You were certainly never that.

Everyone says, 'Well, the French, they are just different'. Having a mistress is just what you do. I wonder, is that true?

When we returned for a visit to our old home in Cornwall after many years away, you said it was painful to return, like meeting up with an old mistress. 'Why would you want to do that?' you said. It jarred a little, that expression you used back then, but now, now, I feel a bit more squeamish about it. It was not hyperbole. It was a reality to you, a feeling you knew only too well.

The problem is that when doubts begin to creep in, they seep into everything.

I was wondering the other day whether it was wise, when you returned to London from France, to work in the same bank as your father. You just kept trailing behind him. The Credit Lyonnaise, a French Bank in London, your father had a senior role there, didn't he? Quite a man to live up to, Dad. I think it must have been tough for you; perhaps you should have tried to do something different to really make your mark. Who knows? It is all well in the past now, but maybe that contributed to the man you became.

I remember you saying you used to wear a black cape over your suit to go to work. How flamboyant. No wonder people thought you were gay. But that is one thing, Dad, we know very well you were not!

I go over and over the stories, looking for the clues that I missed, all the signs that I overlooked, as I loved you so much.

I realise I have regressed to a seven-year-old child; I can hear it in my tone. I feel as if I am the child who had been the only one so far, and the parents come home carrying a new baby. I feel that mixture of resentment, displacement, but also a little wonder too.

I am 57, not 7. How can I have these feelings now? It is as if I had been storing them up and hoarding them just for this moment.

I am not an only child anymore.

My identity as an only child is etched deep. It has been just me for decades.

But now I have a little sister, and I am the seven-year-old I was when she was born, unknown to me, jealous and possessive of my dad.

When this all came out, Mum could sense it, of course, my displacement, my sense of loss of something precious that was mine, and so she showed me pictures of you and I when I was a baby, a toddler, a teenager. Showing them to me like trophies to reassure me, album after album of pictures to make me feel better, to remind me of the life we had led, all that we had shared.

I think nothing broke my heart more than that. Nothing.

That she wanted me to feel ok about it; she wanted to reassure me, like somehow all those good memories had been blotted out, were somehow fake now.

When I stayed with her, she put a photograph in a frame of me in my twenties with you, lounging on the patio, your arm draped over the back of my chair, when I was in my blonde phase. We are both smiling at the camera. She put it on the windowsill to remind me that I have not lost anything.

Can I do the same for her? What of her memories, her stories?

I don't think I want to talk to you anymore, Dad, not for now anyway. The man I loved so much did not exist, and I feel stupid, cheated and lost, you were my anchorage. I still sound like that petulant seven-year-old child. I need to fast forward now and grow up fast.

But just as I want to turn away, I find some hidden letters from you, Dad, to a friend, and I am overwhelmed by your sense of humour and your integrity and all that I loved about you. All the good stuff has come flooding back. I thought I had lost you somewhere. (For those not familiar with the politics of the 1970/80s, CND stands for the Campaign for Nuclear Disarmament. The United States had a nuclear air base at Greenham

Common, at which there was a women's peace camp just outside the perimeter, which was often ridiculed in the mainstream press but became a focus for anti-nuclear protest.)

These were your words:

Kelvin – You mention Greenham Common and your surprise at not spotting Barbara on your tv screen yet. Well, you might actually have spotted Zetta and niece Jane on Easter Thursday and would have certainly identified our car (could you have remembered its appearance?) as it apparently showed up very clearly indeed. Both Helen, Michael and Jane, together with the three of us, are members – I might say passionate members – of CND. On the Thursday in question, I drove Zetta, Jane and a friend of Zetta's to Greenham Common. I was kindly advised by the ladies present that I should 'stay out of things if and when it hotted up' because it is a Woman against the Bomb situation and the mere male must remain an observer (unless he is a policeman, of course). In fact, I found it one of the most moving experiences of my life and have never before experienced such a profound respect for human dignity as I did when watching these brave women in their futile fight for sanity. I'm afraid that the media, as always, has dramatised the odd and the untypical in the Greenham Common scene. Ninety-nine per cent of the women are anything but weirdos or people without respect for others. But you probably realise this anyway. Fortunately, Zetta and Jane escaped arrest – if narrowly – which was a great relief to yours truly. I did not relish having to phone home to advise that these two idiots were ensconced in Newbury Jail whilst I supped the odd beer in the nearest pub. (I would never have dared to go home.)

I have sated myself with memories and stories. I need to deal with the present now. I need to find out about my new little sister. I need to look forward and not look back and find a way to make this right for all of us, those of us left behind, to deal with it.

I have a sister. Gosh, those words sound so strange upon my lips, upon the page. What is she like? Will we like each other?

At least she wants to meet me. Can you imagine the pain if she did not? All these years and then a sister who would remain a phantom, a fantasy. It happens. You read about it. But thankfully, that is not part of my story.

Our story begins now.

Chapter two

THE TEST

I used to have a repetitive thought that on the day of my father's funeral, someone would knock on the door and claim to be my sibling, and it never ended well!

I have no idea what started this thought. Now, in retrospect, I have to wonder if, as a child, I had overheard a conversation that I could not make sense of at the time. People often discuss things in front of children, thinking they will not hear or even understand what is going on. Children pick up so much more than we think.

I had decided I wanted to know if I was more Irish or French, just curiosity, nothing more. So, I ordered a DNA test from Ancestry. Several of my friends had done it and seemed very interested in what they had found out. I did the usual spit into the tube, following the directions carefully, and then I went to put it in the post. As I let go of the package into the postbox, just as it dropped from my hand into the big red pillar box, I had a frisson of fear. What if, what if? No, I said to myself, I was just being paranoid. No what-ifs.

The days and the weeks passed, and I almost forgot about it. Then, one day, the result arrived. Along with the DNA relating to ethnicity, you are asked to give permission for information on shared DNA data with others, something I did without a second thought. When I looked at the results, I found I was more Irish than French, which was much as I had thought. I matched with my father's cousin, Wendy, so there were no worries there. I was his child, phew. I also matched with my mother's cousin, Philip, so I was clearly who I thought I was. All good, or so I thought.

My discovery of a sibling did not come from my DNA test result, but from a test my sister had done with a different testing company. Strangely, she did it at exactly the same time as I did mine. I wonder about such synchronicities; we were obviously meant to find each other.

With my sister's test, she matched with a cousin of my father, who very quickly realised the implications of this, as he recognised her last name as one of a family friend, and he sent both me and my sister a message explaining what this meant to us.

I remember that moment clearly. I was on a train to London at the time, as I was meeting my partner and one of her friends for a concert. I read and reread the email. I could not really take it in. I could hardly interpret the words, it seemed so unbelievable. I remember my heart racing and going into a total fight-flight response, but I had nowhere to run!

When I reached our meeting point in town, I rather anxiously asked if my partner and I could have a few minutes alone, and I showed her the email. She looked at me, eyebrows raised, knowing full well this would lead to all sorts of dramas ahead.

Having shared the information with someone, I felt calmer and a bit guilty for shutting out one of our friends, so we bought drinks, and I explained to her why I was somewhat agitated when I had arrived and had wanted some time alone. Yet another coincidence ensued, as she, too, had the experience of finding out she had a sister she did not know about through her father. I found this profoundly calming and reassuring.

She told me how things had unfolded for her: she had become good friends with her sister, she had pictures on her phone, and I was swept up for a few moments in her enthusiasm for her story. I felt less alone with my experience. There was hope for me to get from this initial shock to a place of safety.

In a way, this experience has informed the writing of this book, as it is not an uncommon experience now with the number of companies doing DNA testing and the proliferation of programmes like *Who Do You Think You Are?* More people find their story is not quite what it had seemed, yet there is little help there. I had some help in the first hours, and I am sure it made this an easier journey for me.

Our cousin, who had contacted us, did try to be as sensitive as he could, saying that we should not judge our parents as they were only human. We must allow them their mistakes. If he had not introduced us to each other, we would have just carried on as before, in blissful ignorance. This worried him for a while, and I know he wondered if he had made the right decision.

In those first few moments, I would happily have rewound time and would have liked to unknow it all, going back to the certainty of before.

Now I know for sure he did the right thing.

Libby Copeland says in her book *The Lost Family* that DNA testing is bringing the past into the present for people to cope with, a past where people faced decisions made in often difficult or even desperate circumstances. I was about to become one of these casualties when I thought the storm, such as it was, had passed.

Copeland cites in her book a research project done by the University of Leuven, which examined how clear the warnings were on DNA testing websites about the risk of non-paternity events occurring, that is, finding out your father was not who you thought he was. The research looked at forty-three English-speaking websites, and it showed that very few sites carried these warnings, and those that did were not very prominent. It is obvious why there are few warnings, as it might cause people to pause before they do the test and decide against it. It would be counterproductive for the companies involved, but of course, it would be far more ethical.

Although I had my twinge of doubt after I had posted the test, I had not considered any wider ramifications before buying it and had not noticed any warnings at all.

The thought to keep in mind is that the results do not just affect you or those who are around now; it is indeed the generations to come. Their sense of who they are may be altered by your discoveries, starting with your own children and then rippling forward. Of course, many people are who they think they are, but it is important to acknowledge that taking the test involves a risk of unexpected revelations.

As soon as I found out, I did what everyone does these days and looked her up on the internet. Her name was familiar to me as our families knew each other, but we had never met. I found a listing on Facebook. I thought it had to be her, and there she was in a picture with two small boys. It had been taken about six years ago.

I stared and I stared at the picture. I thought I could see a shadow of myself in her face, but maybe I was imagining it. Was I imagining it?

Then I looked more closely at the boys, and one wore my father's face. I had been trying to tell myself that it was all a big mistake, but when I saw his face, in that moment, I knew it had to be true.

I copied the image, and I sent it through to my closest family member, who was like a sister to me, a cousin on my mother's side, an only child like me, so she understood what this was doing to me in those early days.

A minute later, a WhatsApp pinged back. She looks a bit like you, she said, and the older boy, oh my goodness, he has your father's face, so it must be true.

Everyone around me was so excited. Oh, amazing, you have a sister.

It did not feel amazing to me; it felt bewildering, surprising, incredible. Overall, it felt unreal.

I felt like I had stepped into someone else's story. I had just found myself in the middle of a BBC2 drama. I did not know my own life anymore. I did not know my lines. I was just standing centre stage with my mouth open and a puzzled look on my face.

We had a hesitant email exchange, not knowing what to expect of each other, and we agreed we needed to be sure. We needed to have another test.

We were very careful with each other, not wanting to cause any offence, saying this was not a rejection, but it was just so big that we had to be sure.

I did one with the same company she had used, and she did one with the company I had used. Belt and braces. We wanted no room for error.

It took nearly six weeks to get the results, though I think I knew it was a foregone conclusion, having seen the photo. Of course, yes, she is my sister.

My father had died before he had to face the music and deal with the situation. He left us in the lurch with so many questions and no one to answer them. We want to know if he knew she was his child and if the man she thought was her father knew. Did any family friends know? Did the grandparents know? Were we the only ones in the dark? As the main protagonists in this story are all gone, we are left just with our questions.

Chapter three

MEETING MY SISTER

Of course, we had to meet for the first time, and it was terrifying, far worse than any first date I had ever been on. In the days running up to it I kept thinking, *I wonder what it will be like? Will we get on? Will she look like me? Sound like me? Think like me?*

Only time would tell.

I was so nervous that day that I changed my clothes at least four times. I had told a friend that I wanted to hit just the right note, not too scruffy, but not too smart, either. I sometimes hide behind my clothes and that would not be appropriate for this special meeting. I needed to be myself, drop the veneer and be authentic.

As I dashed out of the front door and down the road, a shout came from the street opposite: 'That looks just right,' my friend shouted. 'The clothes, I mean, smart casual, just right!' I gave a wan smile and thanked her. What a coincidence she was just passing. Then I dashed on towards the station. I did not want to be late. I am never late.

By then, my clothes seemed the least of my worries as I scurried on down the road. I was going to meet my sister, *my sister*, for the very first time. What strange words those sounded to my inner ear as I said them over and over again, like a panicky mantra.

I was early, of course. I walked past the entrance twice, back and forth, back and forth, like a policeman on patrol.

I tried to peer in at the window to see if she might already be there but could not see, though I was not entirely sure who I was looking for. We should have gone for a carnation in a buttonhole or a copy of the *Guardian* on the table, to be sure.

I took a deep breath and in I went. I stood in the doorway and scanned the room. I was met by a tentative, hesitant, expectant gaze from a face with similar contours to mine, and hair had that waviness at the side that goes so wild for me when the air is damp like today, though she is fair and I dark. There was no mistake. I needed no signs or signals. This was undoubtedly my sister. In that moment, I knew I would fight dragons for her, my little sister; in that moment of recognition, I was there for her.

So here she was. I walked forward. She rose from her seat, and we met for the first time. Yet, I had known this name all my life, being the daughter of family friends.

Now I have seen her, what if I had seen that face before? Would I have noticed, I wonder?

As an only child for 56 years, I have never had that experience of seeing shadows of my face in another, cut from similar cloth but a different style, perhaps that is the way to explain it, and it is so very strange, she seemed so familiar to me, like a long-lost friend.

No wonder we never met before, as there is an instant connection, a recognition. They may have worried we would sense something or maybe recognise ourselves in the mirror contours of our faces. Perhaps.

I wondered what we would say to each other as I took my seat. I very much hoped she was not tee-total because I did not think I could deal with this without a drink. Surely not as a French woman, a glass of wine it must be, a Provençal rosé would be my choice, I thought, as the waitress came to take our order.

My companion said, 'A Provençal rosé, please.' I smiled. It was a good sign. We have at least that in common. We were off to a good start! But that is the thing, the start, how do you start?

Well, it did not stutter, judder, or wobble. It just seemed to flow straight away, like in some obscure way we already knew what we had to say, and for once in my life, I had not rehearsed it, planned it and practised it. I just allowed it to flow naturally.

I guess it says something about the situation for it to be beyond my capacity to create a provisional script for it!

Afterwards, I was wondering whether anyone had been watching us, and if they had, had they conjectured what the story was behind the two middle-aged women who seemed to have met for the first time and were lurching alternately into tears?

Enter stage right. You meet your sister for the first time in middle age. Action!

I plunged in about her brother. Did he know? How did he feel to be only a half-brother now? He did not want to do a DNA test, sheltering in the space of not knowing anything for sure. We ebbed and flowed around who knew. Did he know? She know? They know? Were we the only ones not to know?

How dare they cheat us of a sister, such a precious thing. Of course, we will never know any of that for sure, as her mother and our father are both dead now and the man she thought of as father for 49 years has gone too, so perhaps we park it for now and just get to know each other. So much to catch up on.

She asks if he was a good father to me. She says he was a good man; she says she would describe him as a gentleman. How can I reply? I hesitate to admit he was a good father. It shuts her out. She missed out on this. I do not want to possessively claim this man as my father alone now, that I benefited and she did not from this good and gentle man, but how can I deny it? I do not want to start with lies, so in the end, I say, 'Yes, he was a good father'.

She had worked with him for two years, she said and he taught her all she knew about finance and accounts. All along, he was her father. She did not know. We return to, *did he know*? But could he have hidden it? Not shown a sideways glance, a tender look that would have given the game away or even seemed a bit spooky and weird to this young woman learning her trade. How hard for them both to have missed out on the knowing and the sharing. But at least she knew firsthand that her father was a good man, one who made a mistake, no doubt, but a good man, nonetheless.

There it was in the jawline, the green eyes and the wavy hair.

There are points in the conversation where we just pause and look at each other, not uncomfortable, nor assessing or even questioning pauses, just a sense of being present in this momentous moment.

We stumble into politics. I know not how. What a relief to temporarily move away from the deeply personal, to discover that we share the same values, the passion for our beliefs, the battle against injustice, and the gallic passion to fight for it coursing through our veins. Nature or nurture, will we ever know? Where does one start and the other finish? How they intertwine. Maybe in time, we will unravel it, but time it will take indeed.

We are searching to find similarities between us, questing and digging for them, sifting and seizing upon them like a prospector panning for gold. As we both share a need for belonging, for connections, clearly, our lives may have trodden very different paths, but we have been affected in similar ways and we both crave belonging, family and security. I question if it can be real, this strong feeling I have now to protect the little sister I never knew I had. It feels real, primal, essential to know she is ok and I feel so sad, so very sad when I hear of her struggles at home as a child. I was not there to be her big sister then, but I am there to be her big sister now.

How we wish we knew, if he knew, what we know now. I often wonder why we never met when I knew her brother. Were we kept apart just in case someone noticed any similarities, or we got on really well? No one who is still alive is saying anything, so we will never know.

I wrote the above on the very day I met her. When I got home, I wanted to try to process it through words and it really helped me. It is strange to read it again after a couple of years and imagine how it was to have just met, but that instant connection was so strong I can still feel the pull of it from the page.

I am having to re-examine my view of nature and nurture. You see, she was early, too, and she is obsessed with time just like me and our father. I thought I learned my clock-watching from him, the getting everywhere early with plenty of time to spare, but it seems I did not learn it; I imbibed it in my DNA. Like the political passion and the underlying anxiety, all there written in from the start.

I wonder now how he could have missed it. Not just the similar looks but there is something else there. I recognise her as my sister; there is just a vibe, a feeling, and she worked with him in the office. Could you really have not noticed, not sensed she was his daughter?

I am trying to get to know him again, but it is a bit hard when he is no longer here, and I re-examine our life, looking at it through a different lens. The rose-tinted spectacles have certainly been thrown off, but what do I replace them with?

I wish I could say to him:

It all feels different now. You would be really proud of her. I am proud to call her my sister. But you kept her from me. You took that relationship away from me. And what about her dad? She is having to readjust who she is, and you are not there to help her. Is that fair, really?

I feel for her. It must be so hard to not know who you are anymore, to rewrite the script.

I am just dealing with you keeping secrets from me; that is, of course, if you knew.

Not even a hint, no last confession on your deathbed. With all your religion, Dad, why could you not have told me? I am so hurt you did not trust me with it. It is like you were living a secret life I was not part of, and it makes me so angry, Dad.

Sometimes, we need to find a way to let it out. Say it to a picture, write it down, say how you feel. If you feel something similar, find a way to let it out.

Chapter four

VISITING GRAVES

As the main characters in our story are already dead, which is so frustrating, we felt we needed to visit graves together to find some closure on it all.

We visited our father's grave just a month or so later and I wrote about it straight away again.

I am nervous again. When will that stop, I wonder? I have been working all day, and I need to shift my focus, switch into a different mode. I am in my work clothes still too, no time to change. I feel a little overdressed for this.

We are going to the grave for the first time together. I see her parked up in the street. We smile at each other, and I jump in the car. 'I am nervous,' I say. 'So am I,' she replies. What a relief we feel the same way.

She tells me she has brought flowers; I hear a little hesitance in her voice, silently questioning if this is ok. 'Of course,' I say. 'That is what I had thought you would want to do.'

I must direct us to the cemetery; I am so bad at directions. I do not want the ignominy of getting us lost on the way to our father's grave!

Our father. I have only ever said that in a prayer before. 'Our Father, who art in heaven.' But it is our father now.

So, it is straight along the seafront and then turn right. I have got the wrong road, but I think I can make it right, just a turn to the left, ah yes, straight on now and I see the big wrought iron gates coming into view.

We pull up the car and park. We need to walk the rest of the way. I think I am gabbling inanities. What am I saying? Oh, something about him being buried in a row with some nuns! How very inappropriate under the circumstances.

We walk along the rows of graves, all beloved to someone, and then there it is: *A beloved husband and father,* it reads.

He was my father alone when I had this engraved when I stood here weeping on that summer's day, but he is our father now and forever more. I think I say this out loud. Was that wrong? It is too late if it is. I need to think, think more before I speak.

I see her tears, and I put an arm around her, my little sister. I do not know what to do, what to say, to make this any easier for her.

I feel so helpless.

I suggest we sort out the flowers. She begins to try to get the plastic off; it is not easy, and we wrestle the flowers out together in the end. I think I need to leave her to do this herself, so I head off to the bin with the plastic wrappings and I go to get some water too.

I am crouched over by the water butt, filling an old milk container with scummy water, and I glance over to the grave. She is really crying now, shoulders shaking, heaving. What can I do? Leave her a moment, yes, leave her to have a private moment with him. That is what I need to do. I then, somewhat reluctantly, as I am not sure how long to leave her, head back and bend down to pour the water into the holder for the flowers.

My hand is trembling, and water is pouring out all over the stone as I try to get it into the holes. It makes me think of him, how his hands would shake, and then I stand up rather awkwardly and I put my arm around her shoulders again.

I talk nonsense about what he would be thinking if he could see us together, his two girls united at last.

I think, by the way, that he would be really pleased. He worried about me being left on my own. He used to say so, but if he knew, why not say something? Here we go again; if he knew, could he not have given me a little hint? I wrack my brains. Did he? Could he have?

I just do not know. If he did, I missed it. It passed me right by.

I wish you had, Dad, given me this little bit of hope that one day, one day I might have someone to share the grief with, to share the love for you, to share all the stories, and not bore someone who is just listening out of politeness, but an eager participant in that sharing, listening.

What I find so amazing is how it really feels like she is my sister. I do not have to work at it or think about it. It is just instinctively there.

I wish, I so wish, that I could do something to take this pain away. I can feel it wracking through her body as we stand, side by side, gazing down at the beloved husband and father buried down there.

I stand impotently, hopelessly lost for words to comfort, words to help. Words, they just do not do, are not enough; there are no words, for here and now, maybe silence will do.

Then she begins to tell me about a day when she was just 15 and she headed off with a young man who was much older, who our families knew. They were all worried about her, her mum and her dad, and my dad, our dad now of course. He wanted to know if she was ok, and he went after her, my dad, our dad, and he knocked on the door.

She cannot quite remember what was said, but he showed he was concerned. She thinks she may have been a bit rude to him that day when he went out of his way to check she was ok.

'Oh, don't worry about that,' I say. 'I was rude to him at 15 too. That is what 15-year-olds do. You have got one now,' I say. 'You know how it is.' 'But was he there as my father?' she asks. 'Or the friend of my father?'

I do not know. I wish I could say to her categorically that he was there as her father that day, but we do not know and will never know for sure.

But there is one thing that we do know and that is that he cared for her.

He cared enough to go after her. Can she hold onto this, like a raft on a tempestuous sea, hang on to that, hang on to it? That is all I can offer right now.

As part of getting closer to the roots of the family, it seemed important for my sister to visit some other family graves as so few of our father's family are left alive. So, two years on, we visited our grandparents' grave.

I wait in an overground station at Stratford International for her to arrive. There is no signal on my phone, so I cannot tell her where I am waiting. A sea of West Ham supporters is pouring through the ticket barrier. I worry I will not find her amongst all that maroon and pale blue. The sea builds up to a torrent of football fans bearing her through. There she is with that big smile, so familiar to me now and we hug. I have my two pot plants, and she has her flowers and off we head to the Tube.

We decide to get off two stops earlier than planned, as it looks nearer to the cemetery. We look for a cab when we get out of the station. Nothing in sight, nor minicab office either, and this is London! We Google it and pick one that seems nearest and order our cab. The office says a ten-minute wait and then off we go. When the driver's sat nav tells us we have reached our destination, we are in a suburban street, 'We are going to the cemetery,' we repeat to him. This just cannot be it.

Google appears again and my sister says there seems to be a small path between the houses if we just go back a bit, so we do and there is the path. Off we set, it is very overgrown with weeds and there are discarded household objects and crisp packets littering our way.

It does not seem to be ringing any bells from my previous visit.

We reach a dead end with a signpost in two directions, a leisure centre one way and the town centre the other. No mention of a cemetery. But if we crouch right down and peer behind the sign, there is a fence guarding something. Yes, it is the cemetery just there, but there is no entrance. We investigate and find the fence has collapsed in one place, so we clamber over the railings clutching our flowers and plants and find ourselves in a very old cemetery.

It still does not look familiar, but off we set. I give my sister the map of where the graves are as she is better with maps than me. She turns it this way and that, with a puzzled look on her face. 'This just does not look right,' she says. We stumble about, climbing over collapsed graves and grassy hummocks, looking, searching wildly. 'It cannot be the right place,' I say. 'It is nothing like the one I went to before.'

We roam about looking for an alternative way to escape this godforsaken place than our original trespass, and as we leave, we see a sign saying Wealdstone Cemetery. 'No, no,' I say. 'It is Harrow and Wealdstone cemetery we need. Not this.'

We are now hot, we are tired, we are hungry and most of all, we need a toilet. 'The other cemetery has a toilet,' I say.

Google comes out again. We are not that far from Harrow and Wealdstone Tube. If we head that way, we can get a cab to the cemetery we need. Twenty minutes later, we fall through the door of a minicab office and ask for a taxi to Harrow cemetery. 'Ten minutes,' he says. By then, hunger is almost too much. We met nearly three hours ago. It is now 1.45pm, and we are still clutching our plants and flowers.

We are directed to a cab with the driver sitting eating his lunch from a plate. We ask if there is somewhere to eat near the cemetery. He suggests the Morrison's café. We look at each other with a slight frown. By now, a Provençal rosé beckons and we will not get that there. 'Is there a pub?' I tentatively say. Google presents us with just one, The Royal Oak. It is ten minutes' walk from there to the cemetery. 'That's fine. We can do that when we have eaten,' we say.

We fall into the pub, the toilets first, then to the bar. They have it, amazing, a Provençal rosé. It's the first time we have smiled in an hour. When we order our food, we are told it will be an hour's wait as it's the only place to eat other than Morrisons. 'Not a surprise. We will wait,' we say. As we sit and talk, we drift on to the inevitable subject that always comes up for us – did he know? Did they know? Did anyone know? We don't know, and we never will.

For the first time, though, I can say I feel so sad for him, never being able to acknowledge her, my sister. How hard it must have been when he looked at her and saw traces of perhaps his other child in her face giving the game away, and he had to hold back, stay quiet, even as his grandchildren were born. It is no longer all about me or even me and her. It is also about him. He lost something too.

It is time to leave and resume our journey again.

So, Google again, and we start to walk, and halfway there, I say, 'This just isn't right. This is not the right place,' and we look at the map. It says Harrow cemetery is nearby. No not Wealdstone or Harrow, but Harrow Weald we need. Fifteen minutes by car, Google says.

We call a minicab again, ten minutes, of course, they say. It is now 3.50 pm and it closes at 4.30pm, according to Google. 'Will we make it?' my sister asks. We have two graves to find when we get there. We have been travelling for hours now. We must give it a chance. I am the big sister now. 'Yes, of course we will make it,' I say.

The taxi arrives and off we set. As we get nearer, I realise this is the place. We tumble out of the cab and hit the ground running towards where I think the first grave is. I say that one thing all this drama has done is take the emotion out of this experience. I had been tearful on the train on the way to London, thinking of sharing this with her, but now I just want to get my plants deposited before we get locked in for the night. I cast a glance at the gates on the way in, with their huge rusting padlock, and realise there would be no wriggling our way out of here.

I only just find it; it is so overgrown from the last time. On either side of the grave, we sink to our knees, and she, with her trowel, is trying to pull back the encroaching grass and earth to reveal our grandparents' names. The trowel is cast away, the earth is too hard, and we are now each of us tearing away with our bare hands. There seems something very desperate about our movements, a frantic pulling and tugging to find them there, and gradually their names are revealed. We sit back on our heels and look.

'We would not be here without them, here in this place, here on this earth,' I say. She and I, the result of their meeting all those years ago, before even the First World War. He survived being shot at in the air to come home and become a parent of two, a grandparent of five, if he only knew. I place my plant down, and she her flowers, and we hug. It is so, so good to have someone to share this.

The clock is ticking. No time to wallow in being sentimental; we have not come all this way to find only one grave. Now, we need to find our aunt and her three children, our cousins.

We have to go to a different part of the cemetery and we dash this way and that. I have now lost the map somewhere along the way. We know a number and the area. We dump our bags and our jackets and comb the graves, section by section in different directions. Finally, it is there. The lettering is so faded now that you could almost miss it.

We catch our breath. We sit on the grave, one each side, our aunt and also our cousins, who died at 9, 6 and 3, are down there. We could have known them, shared a life with them, but they were lost to us before we were born. My pot plant goes on the top, and her flowers do too.

None of them are forgotten. It seems important for there to be an outward sign that these long-dead, our family, that they matter to us, and we will not forget them.

But it is time to leave.

We reach those great gates, still open thank god, and yes, another taxi is called. 'Ten minutes,' they say. 'Yes, we can wait outside the gates.' But on examination of the sign it actually closes at 5.30. Google is wrong and we had dashed and ran for nothing.

My phone rings. He is 'At the cemetery,' he says, and we do not seem to be there. He is at Wealdstone, of course, just like we were the first time. 'No, no,' we say and give him the postcode and wait yet again. Then finally, finally, home beckons, and our pilgrimage is done. We paid our respects and got to know each other a little more. Not a cross word or even a bad feeling was shared, during the catalogue of errors on that day, despite the heat and the hunger and the thirst, on our visit to the graves, eighty miles each way and ten hours, gave us just 30 minutes at their graves!

This was, for us, a very important day, one of the deepest bonding moments we have spent together over the last couple of years. Despite it all going wrong, we did not bicker or blame. We laughed and became closer.

Chapter five

A NEW FAMILY

The last of my own personal reflections in the story is of my first meeting with the rest of my sister's family, another of the big hurdles we met about three months in.

'We have got six minutes,' I say. 'That's ok. We do not need to be there bang on the dot,' says my partner. 'Yes, we do,' I say, 'I am never late. My sister is never late.' It is one of those things we have in common that we grasp at to affirm our sisterhood, such new and tender shoots that need nurturing. At least the rain has stopped. We slog along the high street, me speedwalking, my partner trailing resignedly behind, used to my obsession with time. Just five minutes now. Is she keeping up? 'I am here,' she says, and on we go.

I see Rochester Cathedral coming into view, large, dominating the scene. Ah, nearly there, and then, there they are in the distance. I can see them now, a woman and a man and two boys, of course, they are already there, my sister is never late, always early, even earlier than me!

I see her now-familiar broad smile, we are seen, we are welcome, then we are all hugging in awkward combinations, me and him, her and her, here and there.

Greetings are made, and introductions. After all the exchanges, we (that is she and I, my sister and I, forgive me, those words are still so novel) find ourselves standing side by side and the others are ranged in front of us. All in a row, the others stand, and in each set of eyes, we see surprise and recognition; we see them staring, looking from one face to the other, and we look at each other and laugh. We laugh with the joy of it, finding that similarity in one another, that knowing, and yes belonging, unknown still to each other, but belonging, they see it too.

'It is even more obvious in real life than in a photo,' my partner says, as her face cracks into a grin, and then my sister's brother arrives.

I knew him when we were young, our twenties, I guess, but I doubt we could have picked each other out in a line-up these days. So much time has passed.

We have discovered we share a sister; he has one half and I have the other. He is smiling, too. I had been worried about how it would be for him, having to share his sister now with this woman he has not seen for decades, but his smile tells me I am welcome. This is all going to be ok I feel.

What of the boys? I had wondered about this, having nephews for the first time and with some trepidation, would this be how my sons might have looked if I had trodden that path. 'Do you think they look like me?' my sister says. The youngest boy, yes, he has her vibrant smile, a broad face like mine too and a slight shyness around the eyes. Yes, he looks like her.

The older boy, now he, causes me to pause and hesitate. I had seen it in a photo, but in real life, it too is so clear; he wears my father's face, or I say our father's face now.

I am transfixed. It's not just his face, but something in his expression, the slight upturn of the lips, the slightly raised eyebrow and quirky smile. How can it be? It is like being sent back in time to meet my father as a boy, one I had only seen in pictures.

I blunder in and tell him he looks like my father, his grandfather. Not the thing to do, I realise as the words leave my lips. Oh, what a mistake, but it is too late.

He seems puzzled. He was close to the grandfather he thought he had. He does not need another. He is 15. These ins and outs of DNA do not matter to him right now. There is a whole world to explore, and the past does not have that meaning to him, well, not yet, anyway.

So, we begin to walk. My sister and I lead the way, falling into stride side by side, so naturally.

We talk again in animated bursts of how nervous we feel before we meet. 'I think it is fear of losing something so recently found,' I say, and our eyes tear up again.

One of those other things we find we do, almost instantly in unison, the tears do flow, so emotional, hovering just beneath the surface waiting to burst out.

I think of my partner. Is she ok? I glance back over my shoulder, and she is in deep conversation with my sister's brother's wife. Now, that is a mouthful of relationships to unravel! But all is well. She is not alone, and I have time now for my sister.

Goodness, I think. *This is my family, and we are going out for Sunday lunch, and it feels so natural, I feel like I belong here.*

There is that word again. So cherished and tender but easily lost with one false step or so it feels.

Around the table we sit, and the wine flows and the conversations chase to keep up and then the phone comes out for some photos, our first family photos. There is one moment when we catch each other's eyes across the table and we both start to cry again in unison. The others laugh and tease us relentlessly. All is well.

At home later, I pour over the images, yet again, seeing the jawline and the hair. I seem to need constant reassurance that the similarity is there. I am not mistaken. The likeness is really there, and the boys, too, again and again, I look, like an addict chasing a fix, or perhaps just a reminder to myself that I did not just make this all up for my life to feel more complete!

On another day, in those early days, I met her at the station. She turned and looked at me as we greeted each other and I saw my father, our father, in her eyes, just the expression, a look so familiar to me but on a different face.

It took me by surprise. It almost took my breath away, and I told her. I was not sure if I should say it, whether it would make her feel good or bad, whether it was a loss or a gain. She was so pleased; I was glad I had not held it in but shared it. It is good for her to know that part of him, though how I can capture for her that look upon his face on her face, I do not know. But perhaps knowing it is there is enough.

There was an article in the press last week about the actor David Jason. He had just found out he had a fifty-two-year-old daughter and a ten-year-old grandson.

Of course, it brought it all back. Every time you see such a headline, just as you make your peace with it, it all flares up again. It made me think about how my father missed meeting his grandsons. That makes me sad now, but when I first found out, I was so jealous she had given him grandchildren and I did not. It really hurt. It ached deep down. In fact, it was like an old wound that had burst open again.

When I saw the article, I hoped she would miss it. I did not want her to have to think about it again, though I am sure it is never far away. The next day, she mentioned it; it had, yes, it had brought it all up again. At least this woman has a chance of building a relationship with her father. It is everywhere you turn, in TV dramas, films, books and the news. So why is there no template on how to deal with it?

We say it is like you are functioning on two levels. On one, you get it. You understand that this is real. We are sisters, and my father is hers too. But on another level, the denial is still there. It just cannot be true. Just cannot. I tell her stories about the family. The ones he always told me, it seems only fair to share them.

I said to her the other day she is special and it is fine that we are sisters. I am happy with that now, but I am not letting anyone else in, she feels it too, just we two. If any others pop up, it would be just too much. Just us.

Any more metaphorical knocks upon the door and I will not be opening it, or should I say now, *we* will not be opening it.

Enough of my story, our story. What can we do about yours if you're reading this and it resonates with you?

Not everyone is as lucky as we have been and it has not been all plain sailing even for us. We have had to adjust our relationship with the past, with our father and all those around us who lied to us. We have had to learn to incorporate each other into our lives.

The ideas that lie ahead are designed to help anyone who has experienced the shock of a DNA revelation changing their family relationship, whichever position this might be. They also contain useful tools that therapists can use with their clients to help them heal, as there is, at present, so little available to guide therapists in how to help this fast-growing client group.

Part Two – The Therapy Part

HOW TO USE THIS SECTION

This section will explore a range of issues that could be affecting someone who has had their world turned upside down by DNA revelations.

It may be that this directly affects you, someone in your family, or you are a therapist looking for ways to support and understand your client.

Some of the issues that are covered can be experienced by those who have not had such a family shock, as many things can challenge our sense of identity and create shame and blame. And, of course, many families have secrets!

There are different exercises in this section drawn from a range of modalities such as CBT, NLP, Hypnotherapy and Counselling.

There is no 'one size fits all' approach to any psychological healing. You may find that some of the ideas resonate with you more than others. That is fine. If you do not feel the relevance of an exercise, leave it and try another; you can always come back to it at a later stage. Be guided by your needs.

If you are going to do any of the exercises, make sure you have some quiet time in which to do them and a safe space to explore your feelings. You may wish to have a friend with you or work through it with a therapist.

Chapter six

IDENTITY

What do we mean when we talk about identity? Identity is that which marks out the difference between you and me and the billions of other people on this planet. What is unique about you? Who are you? We have a TV programme in the UK called *Who Do You Think You Are?* which reflects the mood of preoccupation with this sense of self in the world these days.

It can be a cause of huge problems if that sense of identity is challenged in some way, and it can be challenged in many ways.

It is a major topic for academics now. This may be because we have more leisure time to consider it, or perhaps this is due to our sense of identity changing through the use of social media. We have this new, wide audience to which we now present ourselves.

Certainly, many are having their sense of identity challenged by widely available and affordable DNA testing. Everywhere you turn, someone has a story of DNA results changing lives; it is the most common plot twist in novels and dramas alike in the early 2020s.

Our sense of identity is important to us. It is something that gives us resilience when we face life's challenges. It provides us with anchorage and brings with it a sense of safety and belonging.

Where does that sense of identity begin?

According to Professor Susan Greenfield in her book *You and Me: The Neuroscience of Identity*, it begins with our name. That is our first piece of the identity puzzle: our personal label. Our first name may be shared with others, but when it is combined with our last name, it becomes who we are; it is the starting point.

This is reinforced now with identity cards and passports that proclaim this is who I am. We can hold it up as proof and validation. If that last name turns out to be false, a parent is not who you thought they were. It challenges that feeling of belonging to the family into which you were born. You have had your fundamental identity feature questioned and that can be so frightening and destabilising. I have an unusual name that is often mispronounced and misspelt. Even on this small level, I can feel frustrated and unable to identify with the name that is being said to me. How much harder that can be if you begin to question that certainty of who you are in a wider way.

Beyond our family name, we have our connection to wider family. Then comes the community around us, then the region and nationality. Though we become more aware of this as we get older, these are the layers of connection that begin from that all-important naming.

Some experts argue that being part of a people is a significant part of our identity. It is a deep-seated part of you, the foundation stone of identity. When discussing identity with friends who grew up in the 1970s, they recounted stories of being out playing with friends and encountering an adult. They would not necessarily ask your name but 'Who do you belong to?' This takes us close to the crux of things: where do we belong? Belonging brings safety. If that is taken away, to whom do you turn? Who will be on your side now? You may feel lost, cast adrift in a force ten gale.

So, what else influences our identity? An important stage of identity comes when we begin to be able to do things for ourselves. When we complete our first self-directed actions, this feeds into our sense of separateness from the adults around us. At around this time, children will also begin to think of themselves as 'I' and have a sense of the separateness of their mother; 'Mummy' is now apart from them and self-actualisation develops.

We then add in our learning. What are we good at? Maybe mathematics, science or languages. This builds our identity. Then there are the wider interests, from playing the piano to surfing or skiing. They all add to that sense of self.

Then we add religion into the mix; politics, sex and sexuality all contribute to who we think we are, and that is the key phrase: who we think we are rather than who we actually are. What about our ethics? What about our values and the roles we play in the world, as a leader or a follower, a mother, a father, a sibling, a friend, a partner or a spouse?

In *The Impact of Identity*, Irina Nevzlin explores the idea that identity is one of the factors we begin to formulate once our primary needs of food and shelter are met as in Maslow's hierarchy of needs. This hierarchy begins with the basic needs, which are physiological, like food, shelter and safety. Only when these are met do we begin to consider the more psychological needs of love and esteem. The last need to be met is self-actualisation, so Maslow is classifying our sense of identity as within our basic needs.

Maslow also states that any thwarting of these basic needs, any sense of threat to them, will be fiercely defended and can lead to what we can define as emergency actions, triggering our fight-flight response. So, this powerful sense of threat needs to be processed to avoid psychological upset and longer-term damage.

We could consider that as we now live in a world where, for most of us, those basic physical needs are met as a given, we are likely to ruminate more on that all-important identity. We have the time to do so, as we are not fighting for our survival. This idea is taken further by Professor Greenfield, who argues that up until the Industrial Revolution, identity was not such an important thing. You were defined by what you did – a farm labourer, a weaver – there was no emphasis on individuality. In the modern world, we are very self-absorbed and looking for ways to assert our individuality.

I would argue there was little time to focus on such things as most people worked so hard that identity was a luxury of the rich in earlier times. Greenfield argues that with the Industrial Revolution came a middle class that began to focus on who you were rather than what you did.

However, I would also suggest that even in the modern world, what you do for a living is used as part of your identity definition. We quickly classify someone by what they do, and it is often the first thing someone will ask you when they meet you for the first time once they have found out your name.

As we have considered, your identity is something you feel rather than something tangible; it is very fragile and easily damaged, as feelings are easily hurt. We can consider mental illness like schizophrenia when someone becomes delusional and their whole sense of self is distorted. Good mental health accompanies a stable sense of identity, though there can be too much focus on being somebody important; we do not want to be nobody. I would suggest that maintaining being 'somebody' is exhausting and the more inflated our sense of identity, the harder it is to preserve it.

So we take ourselves very seriously now. Our identity is something so precious we even discuss identity theft. This is obviously in relation to financial matters, but just hearing the words can make us feel like we want to hold on tightly to that identity. Is that not what we are considering here for anyone who has had a surprise in their DNA test? That they have had their identity taken from them? We may feel there are other ways this can happen: a partner leaves, and they take from you your identity of being in a couple, you lose your job and your identity defined by what you do is stolen. There are many versions of this loss.

We can, however, find new communities on the internet that we can belong to and can use this to enhance our sense of self. This brings new possibilities of belonging. However, Manuel Castells argues that the coming of the internet heralds a me-centred society with a strong sense of individuation. Does this change in our sense of self mean that any challenge to this is more shattering than it may have been before we had social media to enhance our sense of self in such an aggrandising way?

From a neuroscience perspective, according to Greenfield, your identity is, in fact, neurological and is created by your unique connections in the brain, which are dictated by your own unique experiences in life. This is an empowering perspective. If you look at identity in this way, no one can take it away from you. It is yours, your blueprint, eternally yours, yet ever-evolving as new neurological connections and learnings are made.

If we hold too closely to identity definitions of family or job, for example, that we have acknowledged are what we often use to define us, we are making ourselves vulnerable to having that identity challenged and leading to a crisis. But you are more than all of those things. You are you, your unique electrical charges pulsing through your brain, and if we consider the idea of neuroplasticity, you can change and you can adapt.

Nevslin argues that we can learn a lot from immigrants into any new country – how to adapt and change to new situations and create a new sense of identity. They can be a role model for how to hold on to the old, their identity from where they came from, yet adapt to a new environment and become part of a new society. I thought this was an intriguing idea. Is this not what one has to do when one's DNA story changes? You need to accept the family you grew up in, yet also integrate finding your connections to a new family.

Minorities accept the responsibility for their lives and what they make of them when they find themselves in a new community. That adversity makes them stronger, as it requires the need to be more focused. You are no longer on autopilot; you are paying attention to your life and your contribution to it. It ceases to be passive but active and alive. Perhaps, using this idea, we can see the opportunity to grow, to find out who you really are and what you are capable of doing, as you embrace the diversity of your identity.

If you live in another country for a while, you usually feel very much more your own national identity, as one notices all the differences in culture, it makes you more aware of what you thought was just natural. It isn't at all; it feels only natural because in your own country, everyone does things the same way. So, you don't realise that there could even be different ways of doing things, your sense of identity is more activated. This is another example of how our sense of identity can change or be more at the forefront.

Life is not static; we go through stages of development. We are first a baby doing babyish things like playing in a sandpit, then we are a child running around the playground with our friends, then that is too childish, and we stand around trying to be grown up and look cool. We leave school, maybe go to university or start a job. All along, there are changes and we change with each stage, each new input.

There are new jobs, new relationships; change is a given part of human life, one we cannot resist, and do we want to? We are constantly adapting and changing. It provides excitement and fear, which are two sides of the same coin. We can grasp this change in identity however we fit into this new story of family. We can do it with consciousness and work with it. We can stop resisting it but embrace it for the opportunities it may bring.

We clasp familiarity, sameness, as we associate it with safety, but there is no growth in this, and as a species, we have embraced risk to find innovation and enriched lives. Look at what you have achieved in your life so far, the changes you have embraced, the challenges you have met. Is this really going to derail you when you have done so much in your life already?

If you have had a shocking DNA discovery, does it need to shake the core of who you are? You are so much more than the person who is a hostage to their DNA, as DNA is not set in stone. Epigenetics is the area of research which is shining a light on this, showing that our DNA is not as important as we once thought. You can adapt that blueprint beyond the psychological level, even at a physical level. Detail on this is not part of our work, but if you want to learn more about it, Bruce Lipton's book *Beyond Belief* is a good and easy-to-read explanation; you are so much more than your DNA.

If we ask ourselves what identity is, is it our basic DNA that we were born with? Or that blueprint of connections in the brain that develop over time? Is it our collection of memories, our jobs, lifestyles, tribes, nationalities, skills, hobbies, friendships, life roles, values, religion, beliefs?

It is all of these things, so if one element of that package needs to change, it does not need to derail us completely. The most amazing thing about the human condition is its ability to adapt. It can adapt to a new environment and new life situations; that is how we survive, so now is the time to adapt wherever you fit in your DNA story, and I have some exercises further on that will help you to do this.

We can also consider, before moving further, how we can pay too much attention to our sense of self, as detailed earlier. Previous cultures saw the threat of this and worked at strategies to move away from it. The more we invest in the self, the more vulnerable we can be, yet it can give us some resilience, as we have already considered. In Buddhism, for example, nirvana can be interpreted as an emptying of the self, which is the highest point of ecstasy. Nothing can be taken from us in this state, we just are. Can you imagine the peace of not trying to constantly defend that precious sense of self?

It may be that if you are less aware of self, challenges to your parentage or family make-up will affect you less. The practice of mindfulness used in all early spiritual traditions from Hinduism, Buddhism, Christianity, Islam and Druidry all move the focus into the moment and what you are experiencing, which takes you away from who you are. If we come back to neuroscience, a similar state can be obtained when moving from mind into sensation by immersing oneself in loud music or doing a sport like skiing or surfing; even sex takes us away from the self. We are no longer self-conscious; we are abandoning ourselves to the experience and we find some inner peace away from this individuality, this self.

We can have moments of escape from ourselves through such action, but we cannot be constantly trying to find ways into sensation and out of cognition. We can also find some mindful peace at times in meditation, but in the modern world, to reach this sense of disconnection for long is hard, so one of the exercises at the end of this chapter is designed to help you gain some balance in your identity and not have too many eggs in one basket.

We touched on social media and its impact earlier, and we will explore it a little deeper now. In *The Psychodynamics of Social Networking* by Dr Aaron Balick, the author argues that we now have two identities that we face to the world in our social media postings: the more real and authentic self, which perhaps our close friends and family observe. This adds a complicated new layer to understanding ourselves, and we may even become confused about who our real selves are. Of course, we are a complex mix of these outer and inner identities, though there can also be a blurring between fantasy and reality.

Our sense of self is somehow expanded in social media. We could even say that the sense of self that social networking has created is verging on narcissism.

Brené Brown also tackles this subject in her book *Daring Greatly*. There is a perception that people think what they are doing is so important that the world needs to know about it, down to what they ate that day. People have become very 'me' focused and Brown quotes some research in popular music that notes a shift away from the words 'we' and 'us' in songs towards 'me' and 'I', which is a fascinating way to track this shift in perception.

Why is this important for our area of interest regarding changes in our birth family? Or, indeed, any of many challenging life situations? Well, the more obsessed we are with our sense of self, the more vulnerable it is to any sense of threat to it.

If our sense of belonging that creates this foundation of identity can be challenged through social media, i.e. if we are not connecting or being 'liked' by who we expect to be, or our life does not seem as exciting as our so-called friends' lives, many of whom nowadays we have not even met, we are vulnerable.

If our sense of self is more based on a fragile edifice like our social media presence or what people think of us than a change in our belief in who we are, we are more likely to break down. We feel publicly exposed, perhaps even when the change in our situation is not widely known yet, as we are more used to being in the spotlight. We are expecting judgement and censure. The bigger our sense of self, the harder we fall. The less solid the foundation, the more it will shake.

The concept of an 'identity crisis' is discussed by James Fearon at Stanford University in his paper 'What is Identity?' The term 'identity crisis', first coined by Erikson, refers to changes in the concept of the self in regard to character and beliefs. It specifically refers to origins in this context, and though he says it is most relevant in adolescence, he does acknowledge that it is affected by what he calls disruptive conditions, and what could be more disruptive than finding out you were not who you thought you were? I think anyone going through a non-paternity event will experience an identity crisis of some sort; its severity will depend on how entangled with family the identity had become.

I am devoting quite a lot of time to this idea of identity, approaching it from different angles and ways of understanding it, as it is so crucial to our sense of well-being and is so easily crushed.

It builds and it builds over time, layer upon layer, added to that sense of who we are. To fully understand the importance of it, we could imagine waking up one day with no memory of who we are and how that would feel. How do we engage with the world around us without the shield of identity?

Whilst researching this chapter I came across the Netflix documentary *The Remarkable Life of Ibelin*. It is the story of a young man who suffered from

Duchenne Muscular Dystrophy and died aged 25. The last years of his life were spent in a wheelchair with very limited movement. After his death, his parents discovered that he had a completely secret online life in the game *World of Warcraft*. In this, he could walk, run and live a full life. He had a romance that he could not have in his real life. He had formed deep relationships with other players and his parents realised he was not the lonely young man with a constricted life experience they had imagined. He had this rich other life.

As I watched this, I considered we were again dealing with an issue of identity. Ibelin had reinvented himself and found happiness, albeit in an imaginary realm, but the connections he made with others were real and he had built up self-esteem and had adventures he could never have experienced due to his disability. This surely challenges our sense of identity and what defines who we are. Who was the real Ibelin? Was it the one in the game or the young man stuck in his wheelchair? I would argue he was both. This makes us consider that we can move beyond our limitations and our beliefs if we feel our identity is challenged. I am not suggesting we all disappear into a world of fantasy. In fact, I think it is very important to keep a foot strongly planted in the real world, or we can begin to drift towards dissociation from reality and mental illness, but we can begin to reinvent ourselves. We are not stuck with the limitations we often perceive. We are so much more than where we came from. We can remake ourselves with the right tools.

In my own personal story, I see the upset in my sister trying to rewrite her story, trying to adjust her sense of who she is now. My story has changed too, more subtly, but I spent 56 years of my life identifying as an only child, a small thing in the greater scheme of things, but my identity has changed. I have also become an aunt. I have only been an honorary aunt in the past, so I need to rewrite my sense of identity.

At first, I was aware that I felt like a typical first child when the second child arrives, and I was facing this in my 50s. I had had my father all to myself for decades and at first I did not want to share him. Although he is already dead, I have still had to learn to share his story with my sister and share some of the things that belonged to him. I have had to learn to say, 'our dad' rather than 'my dad'. It was very hard at first. I felt like I was behaving like a spoilt child throwing a tantrum when I found out – not an edifying image, especially for an experienced therapist. If I find it challenging, how hard it must be when you face greater challenges to your sense of who you are and, of course, the other people around you.

How much your sense of self is affected will depend on your 'locus of control', that is, how much you feel you are in control of your destiny and how much you feel you are swept away by chance and the events that happen to you.

If we believe we have no control over our lives, we become fatalistic, hopeless and tossed about by the whims of fate on the sea of life. This is known as having an external locus of control. If we believe that despite what might happen, we can influence the outcome or at least control how we respond to it, then we have hope of recovery. In this case, we have an internal locus of control.

You may be in a position now where your life has been turned upside down. You can stay in this state of flux, allowing this life event to define you; you can worry about what others may think, how this affects who you are, or you can choose to take control of this life experience, take an internal locus of control and see what you can make of your new life.

Of course, there are many events in life that may challenge your sense of identity, and the exercises may help you (however this has come about) to take control of the impact of any life event.

In this chapter, the exercises are designed to try to help you build up your sense of self in a balanced way if it has felt under threat in any way. Now is the time to create who you want to be based on all that you have learned.

Exercise
Word map

I would like you to work with the idea of creating a word web relating to your sense of identity. This idea is useful for anyone to practice creating a well-grounded self.

What you need to do is draw a large oval in the centre of a page, write the words 'My Identity' in the middle, and then draw a series of lines branching off from the oval. At the end of each line, name something that contributes to your sense of identity, some of which we have already referred to, like nationality and job; even the way we dress may reflect something about our sense of self, the group to which we feel we belong.

Really let your mind focus and think about all the different things that affect your sense of self. You may want to write a list first before filling it out on your web.

When you have completed your map, on a separate piece of paper, draw a large circle and divide it up into segments like a pie chart or pieces of cake, making each represent one of the factors contributing to your sense of identity, so some slices of the circle will be bigger than others. Working out the major and minor influences on your sense of self may take some thinking time. The important thing is to be really honest with yourself about it. If you want to, you can do this a few times until it feels like you have the distribution right.

Now look and see what you can learn from this. Do you need to adjust your emphasis? I do not mean on paper now, but do you need to alter the influence of certain things on your sense of self? Perhaps you place too much weight on your relationship, so if that were to go wrong, then your identity would be derailed.

Considering how much more there is to your sense of self brings safety and security if one element is affected, challenged or changed.

It may be a smaller change you have experienced. DNA has shown you that perhaps your nationality has other influences than you thought, or maybe even none at all. This exercise is important to create a balanced sense of self.

So, to recap, the two key areas are:

Look at the range of factors involved in your sense of identity, and if you are not coming up with a range of influences, you might ask yourself why. Consider whether you are putting too much emphasis on one area, and if possible, could you broaden out your sense of self?

By actively engaging in this practice and giving it your attention, you are already affecting change, as that which is observed is, at a quantum level, already changing. It is so empowering to work with who you are; it is not fixed and static. It can evolve.

Exercise
Questions

It may be helpful to ask yourself some key questions about how your sense of self evolved. We can then help build your identity with the following questions:

What do you do that you feel defines you in the outer world? Is it your job, your education? Your marital status? Being a parent?

What are your attitudes and behaviours, even particular styles, that you may feel define you?

How does your gender affect your sense of self? Is it a key factor or did it not even make it onto your word web?

Do you classify yourself by your age? Is that important to you?

Do you feel a kinship for people of your own age group?

What about your cultural background and where you grew up? Your nationality? How does this influence your sense of self? Is it a strong part of your identity?

What big life experiences do you think have influenced what you believe in and who you are, if any?

Do you have any special interests and hobbies? If so, how do these affect your sense of who you are? Do you connect strongly with others with the same interests or just a small amount?

Can you think of four core values that govern your life now?

Core values are things like empathy, efficiency, reliability, determination, honesty, accountability, authenticity, dependability, carefulness, loyalty, thoughtfulness, fairness, consistency, tolerance, sharing, and self-control, to name but a few.

Have those values changed over the last ten years? If so, what do you think has influenced that?

Are there aspects of how you see your sense of identity that you would like to change?

Having answered these questions, who are you really?

Would the real you stand up, please?

Exercise
Self-appreciation

If your sense of self has been challenged recently, we need to focus on all that is good about you, moving away from criticism and building on your strengths. We have considered what you want to change, but what do you want to keep? This exercise will help you if you look at yourself from an alternative perspective. It involves seeing someone who cares for you; it does not need to be a partner or family. It can be a friend or neighbour, even a pet.

I would like you to imagine that you are walking along a corridor and looking at a series of doors. You pick a door. Notice how it feels to turn the doorknob in your hands and enter a beautiful room, rather like an old-fashioned library.

But first, notice the colours upon the walls are soothing and that there is a roaring fire in the grate, make your way over to it, watch the colours in the flames as they dance. I wonder if you can hear the crackle of the flames as they pop and crack as the smoke rises up the chimney.

There is nothing for you to do right now so sit down in front of this fire, staring into the flames and you can begin to relax, you are not thinking about anything specific, just noticing the comfort of the room, sitting in a cosy, comfortable armchair, feeling it supporting you, sinking down into it and enjoying the peace and calm you can feel in this room.

You notice that there are bookshelves upon the walls, all your favourite books, your favourite stories, tales of heroes and heroines from the past, from the present. There are paperbacks, hardbacks and old leather tomes with gilt-edged pages, so many books, so many stories.

You scan the titles as best as you can from where you sit.

Now, you are here for a reason. Though relaxing is the first step, you need to consider that you have been asked to write a resume of your best qualities, and you are lost in thought, unable to focus. What are your best qualities? We all have things we are good at. Everyone has and so do you. You are so much more than your family and where you came from. Who have you become?

Now, you get up from your comfy chair in front of the fire and see a desk, somewhere you can sit and write this list easily. You may not have noticed this desk at first, so absorbed were you by the books and the fire, but now you settle down into a desk chair where paper and pen await you. Feel the pen in your hands, get the sensation of it and begin to write about who you have become, the best things that you have done, the things you are proud of; these things contribute to who you are.

When you have written all that you can think about this list, gaze about the room, enjoy the comfort there. You see that outside the window watching you is someone who cares for you, not family. This is a friend/colleague or partner and you can see a smile in their eyes as they look in at you, waiting to join you in the room. You can see affection in their gaze. They know all that is best about you; that is why they are your friend or partner.

I would like you to stretch this powerful imagination of yours a little further and see yourself float out of your body from where you sit, float out of the window and into the person who cares for you. Look through their eyes; look at you through their eyes. Why do they choose to be in your life? What are your strengths to them? See yourself in the light of their eyes. Your parentage or anything your family has done does not affect anything they think of you. They know you and know you are so much more than this, from where you came from. They know who you are now.

What do they see? What would they write about you in this resume of your best qualities?

Focus your mind on their thoughts, seeing yourself through their eyes.

Think of at least five sentences that they would say about you as they look at you, your strengths, your best qualities.

Now float back, back into your body, relaxing in that comfortable room, the chair at the desk, and write down on the piece of paper on the desk. Take your time; there is plenty of time and you can return to the exercise any time you want to add to this new sense of you, through others' eyes. That's right.

Now, when you are ready, and only when you are ready, come back to the words here on the page and leave the room behind, aware of where you are in time and space right now. That's right, holding onto the words on the page.

Some people struggle with floating into the image of a loved one. If this is hard for you, just imagine there is a picture of a loved one looking at you from a photograph somewhere in the room. This may be easier to imagine. It can be someone from any time in your life. I mentioned a pet in the introduction, as even a pet can have a feeling of appreciation. Maybe just getting the feeling of being cared for is what is needed at this time, rather than focusing on qualities which are just as powerful for building self-esteem.

Once you have done this exercise in your imagination, you may wish to really write down on a piece of paper all you learned from this experience.

You could add to it by asking some friends what they like about you, why they choose to spend time with you and add to your list.

Exercise
Anchoring the self

Anything that threatens our sense of identity or sense of belonging makes us feel less secure. We have been looking at ways to build on our sense of self and our strengths. We need to find ways to make this tangible for you, for you to feel more secure and grounded, so we are looking at a way here to anchor that sense of self.

Before we go into this exercise, we need to consider the role of metaphor in healing. It has been used for centuries to bring learning and understanding to our unconscious mind, that part of our mind that holds our memories, habits, behaviours and emotions.

If this is a new idea to you, it is important to recognise how we take in information, how words can be so much more powerful when our senses are engaged and how we have, since the earliest time of mankind, learned through stories.

You may notice that if I say, 'I can see the light at the end of the tunnel', it is more powerful than saying, 'things are getting better'. Engaging with the imagery makes the first sentence so much more powerful for you to relate to.

When creating metaphors for therapeutic use we also use rhyme, rhythm and pacing so that it becomes almost poetic, so the idea we want to understand weaves its way into the mind without resistance or avoidance.

The story creates the connecting strategy between one idea and another. We want that eureka moment of understanding that this idea is about me; it speaks to me.

Stories provide us with a safe way to explore new ideas.

I am going to provide some different metaphors for you within the exercises to read through and visualise to help on that road to healing. It may help to record the words, close your eyes and listen.

Sit in a place where you can be quiet and undisturbed for a while……….take a deep breath and release it… releasing the tension you are holding in your body…… any tension that, considering the change in your story, is creating for you…..pause this for a moment or two.

I would like you to go on a journey with me….a journey in your mind…….following my words….. letting go of the thoughts of everything that has happened so far today and everything that is yet to come….leave that for now and stay with the images we will be working with today.

I would like you to imagine a mountain……. an image of a mountain in your mind…..if it is not easy for you to see images in your mind….just sit with the idea of the mountain…the thought of the mountain….. it could be a mountain you know…….one you have seen in a picture or…….a mountain created by your mind………..your imagination…….as you drift deeper and deeper into relaxing….just focusing on the idea of the mountain….

This is your mountain……. it belongs to you…..no one can take this away from you….you are in charge….. it is all yours…..I wonder what your mountain looks like?…..Does it have more than one peak?…….It may have some trees on its side…….are there trees scattered across the slopes?…….perhaps with branches waving in a gentle breeze?……..

Is the mountain capped with snow?………..are there pathways weaving up the sides?…………..is there a stream weaving its way down, bouncing over boulders….. rocks and pebbles?…just think about the idea of the mountain….clouds perhaps hovering around the top of the mountain.

This is your mountain…….anchored to the earth……a part of everything, but standing strong and grounded……. just like you now…feeling stronger and grounded…. that's right…

You have done some good work to reevaluate that sense of identity….you are grounding that now….you are so much more than your parentage…is that not a circumstantial accident?….

That biological parentage is a circumstantial accident….whether planned between two people or not….it is always chance….why does one egg fertilise and one not….the role of the dice and here you are……but that is just the beginning……what you have done with your life…the things you have learned and done….the relationships you have cultivated….they are who you are….you are so much more than your parentage or where you were born….

Notice the mountain again…stay with it…..notice it has sloping sides….the sloping sides of the mountain…..a still mountain……a peaceful mountain……now I would like you to think about bringing the image of the mountain into your body……

You are the mountain……..the peak is your head and the slopes your shoulders and arms……..standing firm and tall and strong within your landscape…….being mountain……..feeling the strength of being mountain……..

The earth is anchoring you……..it is solid beneath you…….the solid foundation of your being….realising now the solid foundation of your being…..

Breathing as mountain……some warm spring rain may land upon you…………that light spring rain pattering upon the ground… upon you….splashing in the stream that is winding down the sides of the mountain…..

Storms may come……..like the storms you have experienced that shook your sense of who you are….the information…new knowledge that troubled you at first…..or any other difficulties in life…..it may make the trees sway………it may make the water race………

But the mountain stands………you stand……… feeling the storm pass…….the sun come out………the warmth of the sun on the mountain………the warmth of the sun upon you……..feeling the day pass in the warmth of the sun……….aware of who you are now…. all that is you…strong with this new awareness of your sense of self…that important self-actualisation….. you know who you are now….that will just get stronger and stronger now….

And watching the sun slip down in the sky……….as you sit as mountain……….as you breathe as mountain………as the colours of the sunset dance in the landscape…..the oranges and yellows and pinks…. feeling the solid strength of mountain…..storms come and storms go…….the rain comes and it goes……… the sun comes and it goes…….then it is spring and the new small plants break the surface of the soil……a snowdrop perhaps……

The promise of spring in the smell of the air and the bright colours of summer are there…feeling summer for the mountain……..as you breathe as mountain…….. the colours of summer…..is there heather on the sides of your mountain? ….is there yellow gorse?……….

Then we roll into autumn…the colours change to rusts and browns….you may notice clouds passing by casting shadows across your mountain……

What does it feel like, I wonder?…..being the mountain….sitting as the mountain….the moon rising as night falls….the moonlight falling upon your mountain…..so now it is winter… colder…. snow….. hail storms….crashing into your mountain…..but now you are so much stronger…you can deal with this now….

The mountain is sitting untroubled by what is happening upon the surface…strong through the changes of the season whatever they might bring…. because after those storms of winter…the cold of the winter…..spring is around the corner….the light and the dark….the happiness and the sadness….our storms come and go…..constant change like the changes in the landscape….but we can sit as mountain with a gentle acceptance…an inner strength within that we can find as mountain….

So, stay for a while sitting within the awareness of mountain, the changes in the landscape….enjoying the peace that comes with being mountain….that's right.

In this exercise, we are building a sense of inner strength, inner reserves that perhaps one can too often ignore as they can be hidden beneath stress. It encourages one to look inside for strength rather than outside, thus creating greater resilience and less dependence on people and material supports to make us feel safe as if one relies on inner resources, they are less easily compromised. It is also important to look for a point of stillness when life feels unstable and insecure. This exercise helps to achieve this.

Chapter seven

SECRETS AND LIES

We are starting this section with secrets and lies as if you or someone you know have had a surprise DNA result, then someone has been keeping secrets and perhaps also telling lies.

Secrecy is dangerous. It leads to a lack of trust and doubt. Doubt is like a worm burrowing into a healthy apple that goes on to wreak havoc within. When we are not being told the truth, a sixth sense, perhaps powered by our subconscious mind, knows about it and leads to confusion and struggle, trying to understand what is real and what is not. As I have referenced in my own case, even as children, we pick up on so much more than adults give credit for. Through body language and tone of voice, we have an instinct for when things are being concealed from us.

We can then find ourselves doubting our instincts, our place in the family and the adults around us, even perhaps other siblings, wondering if they know something we do not.

The truth is something we can deal with whatever it brings us. Not knowing the truth is poisonous, as our fears may turn out to be worse than reality. Children can be so much more resilient to the truth than they are to the lies they are told. Adults hold conversations in front of children who are perhaps sleeping in the back of the car or dozing on the sofa, assuming that as they are not fully alert, it will not affect them. But although the conscious mind may not be engaged, the subconscious mind is always listening and absorbing what is going on around it.

Many families have secrets; the issue is how big the impact of their revelation will be on those who have been kept in the dark. Secrets also take a toll on the person or persons holding the secret; it is one of those commonly held beliefs that sharing a secret will relieve the burden of carrying it. This can be seen when a criminal wants to confess a crime or be caught just to relieve the burden of the secret.

Research done by Nir Halevy at the Stanford Graduate Business School and Adam Galinsky at Columbia Graduate School into the challenge of carrying a secret found people felt both fatigued and isolated when they were faced with holding a secret rather than information that was widely available. The conclusion from the research was that it is one of our primary instincts to connect with other people, but if we are holding onto a secret, it makes us feel isolated. We need to keep more separate for fear of revealing the secret, thus creating an inner conflict of drives between connection and safety, as our safety depends on keeping the secret.

Of course, good secrets can be as challenging to keep too, such as buying a present for someone.

You know they will really like it, but having to wait until their birthday or Christmas to give it to them, you are so excited to see their reaction you almost want to spoil the surprise and tell them the secret.

Research by Edy Moulten-Tetlock discovered that revealing a secret to just one other person lightened the load of carrying the secret, as it reduced the amount of time the person spent focusing on it, and usually, the carrier of the secret received support from the listener. By doing this, they are also now, of course, sharing the responsibility of keeping the secret.

We may have all been in the position of holding a secret for someone and having to remind ourselves constantly that it is not to be revealed. We can see that this is very draining and takes up a lot of mental space, along with, of course, the fear of responses to that secret if it were revealed. The research concludes that it is mainly the preoccupation with the secret, the rumination over that secret, that causes the psychological damage, making the secret holder feel trapped.

We are considering the toll on the keeper of the secret to bring some perspective on the situation, as if secrets have been kept from you, it will have taken its toll and we do need to acknowledge that secrets hurt both sides of the secret equation.

Interestingly, Sisella Bok states that secrets can debilitate judgement. This is an interesting thought because if we know all the information available, we can make an informed choice, but if there are secrets involved, we are not making our decisions based on all the information and this can lead to erroneous beliefs. It creates an abuse in relationships due to the inequality of information. If a secret is revealed, then trust between individuals can be destroyed and secrets can lead to people feeling like an outsider if they have been kept in the dark about something, perhaps even feeling ridiculous if they have made decisions based on incorrect information.

I can have a client in deep trance who will tell me after the session that they cannot remember anything I said and felt they had not heard anything, yet the moment I asked them to open their eyes, they did. I use this explanation to help them to understand that their subconscious/unconscious mind is always on duty. Of course it is, as that is what keeps you safe whilst you sleep and will wake you if it hears a strange noise in the night or if you feel unwell.

With this in mind, I come back to the information shared in front of a sleeping child. What might you have heard the adults around you say to each other whilst you slept? You may have no conscious memory of it, but if that lower part of your mind heard something, it may have fed a feeling of unease, of not belonging, perhaps, a feeling about which you could never quite identify the origins.

I have already referred to my lingering questions about whether I had a sibling that could have come from instinct or something more practical. Copeland refers to these family secrets revealed through DNA in her book as secrets that have been frozen, only to be thawed out decades later rather like a caveman frozen in the ice. She refers to the stakes being high when you spit into the bottle! These secrets, when thawed out and revealed, hurt so many people. They ripple out into the family, leaving a trail of casualties. However, there are those who feel the truth is easier to deal with than the feeling that there are secrets hidden in their background, like a shadow, always there, but it is not possible to see quite what it is, so you cannot begin to process it.

Gabrielle Schwab says in her book on generational trauma that we cannot fight shadows. We cannot deal with what we do not fully know. If we face the truth, we can begin to heal. It is not a magic fix, but there is hope of healing rather than this festering secret that feeds distrust and causes confusion.

Each individual will respond differently. For some, it is a relief to know. For others, they may wish they had never known. For me, denial felt like the first port of call, but now I know my new family, I am glad that we do know. I wish we could have met sooner, but it takes time to reach this place for many, if they reach it at all.

We cannot really examine the idea of secrets without considering the accompanying actions of lies and omissions that can go with them. The expression always recalls to me the powerful film *Secrets and Lies*, made in 1996 and starring Brenda Blethyn as a mother whose adoptive child seeks her out. The humour and pathos of this story are so powerful and it explores many of the dynamics that we are examining in this section of the book.

Lies can be direct or lies of omission, and I think in the case we are dealing with, the majority will have faced lies of omission. Not many of us would have had the courage to ask outright, 'Is my father my real father?' 'Am I really an only child?' or, 'Do I have half-siblings out there?' even if we had wondered about it. The questions may have crossed our minds, but perhaps fear of the answer holds us back. We do not want to really know the truth as then we have to deal with the consequences, so we can find ourselves colluding in a lie, something we may later chastise ourselves for doing. We may also hold back due to loyalty to the parent whom we see as also betrayed in the situation. The betrayal bonds us to the other parent, even if they are not the biological parent. Our motivations in this situation are very complex, but at the root of it lies a need for safety.

In Sissela Bok's book, *Lying*, she addresses directly the issue of being lied to about parentage and the ensuing resentment, disappointment in a trusted figure and the feeling of having been manipulated, how it brings reflection on the past through a new lens. This can, of course, lead to distrust in all close relationships from then on.

Lies have consequences for both parties. Living with a lie for many years and fearing the consequences of exposure is exceptionally wearing. Most of us have at some time told a small lie and felt the weight of it. Imagine carrying a lie in such an important matter as parentage. The liar does not come out of this unscathed in the same way as the holder of secrets. The liar may repeatedly justify the lie to themselves, but the accompanying fear, in most cases, will be very eroding.

One thing to consider is, if the lie had not been exposed, would life have felt better or worse? Do you sometimes feel you wish you had not found out? If so, this may be a tough acknowledgement. The lie was told to a certain extent to protect you. This is often defined as a paternalistic lie as someone is deciding for you and for your best interests as they see them, though there is usually some underlying self-service at work and paternalism is a part of the self-justification.

As children, one of our fundamental learnings is to tell the truth and therefore not to lie. We may have wrestled with guilt as small children about any number of small misdemeanours 'No, it was not me,' etc. How challenging in later life, after trying to be honest and live up to our parents' expectations, to be faced with hypocrisy on this level. I think this underpins the feelings of betrayal. The parent is meant to be the role model for life, and the model was flawed. The parent was meant to protect us and yet they have created considerable pain through their actions.

Lying is an active choice, and it comes loaded with responsibility towards the person or persons you are deceiving. Though most liars do not expect to be revealed and the longer the lie goes on, they can sometimes even begin to believe the lie themselves.

My parents' generation could never have imagined that ordinary people would have access to DNA testing and that the lie of omission, engaged in decades ago, would be revealed. In my case, the key players in my story are all dead, so they have not had to deal with the consequences of their actions, and this leaves us with so many unanswered questions. The whole truth is not and never will be available to us, which is a huge challenge and compounds the feelings of deception.

Kubler Ross addresses the concept of secrets in her work with grief. All families have secrets and often they come out when someone dies. But even if in your situation, a bereavement is not part of the story, the effect of the secrecy is still there. The feeling that someone has withheld something from us is personal to us, and we often feel others must have known and it was just us left in the dark.

It feels like an insult to the relationship that the information was not shared and confers a lack of trust. It makes the relationship seem belittled and altered through the secret and it raises so many questions in its wake. If the person who withheld from you is still alive, then you have an opportunity to process this more easily.

If they are already dead, as in the case with my family, our biggest challenge is the not knowing, not knowing who knew what and how much we were kept in the dark. Was it just us, my sister and I, or did the secrecy go wider? Somehow it feels more painful if you are the only one who is not party to the secret. It leaves behind feelings of sadness and betrayal.

Exercise
Keeping secrets

It is hard to keep a secret. If a secret has been kept from you, it may help to consider the toll doing this may have taken on the keeper of the secret.

Think of a person you would often mention in conversation at work or with friends. It could be a partner, a child or another family member. For one week, do not mention them at all. If someone raises them with you, then change the subject; just see how it feels to have something important to you that you cannot discuss.

You might want to make notes about how this felt once you have completed the exercise and note if it has brought you any insights.

Exercise
Telling lies

Everyone tells lies at some point in their life, sometimes small lies that seem irrelevant, and sometimes we try to make ourselves feel better about it by calling them 'white lies'. But often we get a sense when we are being lied to and it sows the seed of distrust and uncertainty. It is interesting to test your instincts, and it may inform feelings about when you may have felt you were being lied to in the past.

Get together with a friend and pick a time in your life you want to discuss with them. Do not decide this in advance; pick it when you sit down to talk. Tell them about this time in your life, but insert one lie. Tell them they need to identify the lie when you have finished talking to them.

Then do the same the other way around with your friend telling you about something in their life and inserting one lie. I wonder how you felt telling the lie and if you were detected. Did you feel uncomfortable, a little embarrassed telling the lie or maybe not? Can you easily detect a lie?

This can be an interesting exercise to try a few times to understand that telling lies brings feelings with it; even when you are doing it in this kind of game, there are consequences to lying. It is also interesting to discover if you have a sense when people are not telling you the truth. Some people become so used to being lied to that they end up being unable to trust anything anyone says to them. This is a sad outcome of this pattern of deception.

You may wish to write down what insights this exercise has brought to your family situation.

Does the feeling of detecting a lie or telling a lie feel familiar? Have you had this feeling before in your life? To what situation is it attached? When did you feel it the first time?

Chapter eight

EMOTIONAL STATES – BLAME

If we are suffering with physical or emotional pain, we can move into a place of blame. If we sit in the blame of somebody or something else for our pain, it makes us feel we have done something about it, passed responsibility to someone else. It is their fault, so in some way, it is their responsibility to resolve it, not ours.

It is, in a sense, a very passive state; I pass the blame to you, and I sit in my suffering. As in many situations, especially the one we are considering, there is not a great deal the figure of blame can do to alter your pain. They can, of course, apologise. This may help, but it does not alter the situation in which you find yourself.

It is a totally natural defensive response, but it traps us.

It feels like you are taking action by passing and attributing blame, but as the figure of blame cannot resolve it for you, it bounces back to you.

You find yourself still feeling bad, nothing has changed. We need to take action to heal, and that action needs to be positive action if we want to find our way out of the pain. If you feel wronged and hurt, one thing to consider is, were you the target of this act?

Did someone deliberately hurt you? In some situations, this may be true, but if we apply this blame to the action of your parent having been unfaithful and producing a half-sibling, or you find yourself not to be the child of a parent, this was not targeted at you, it was not done to hurt you.

You are caught in the fallout; you are a casualty of this perhaps irresponsible act, but not the target.

One of your parents, or indeed both, have made mistakes. At some point, once they made their mistake, they made decisions to try to mitigate that mistake, which may have made things worse through secrets and lies, as we have examined.

But we need to question whether sitting with this blame is moving you forward or keeping you stuck; the exercises below may help you resolve this.

I am not suggesting moving from a place of blame straight to forgiveness. That is a big leap. But finding ways to move out of blame will be empowering for you; it is part of the journey to healing.

Exercise
Drop down through model

We are going to examine a technique here that can be useful to transform your emotional responses or emotional behaviours. It is an adaptation of the 'Drop Down Through Model' which has its origins in CBT.

So firstly, we need to look for the negative emotion. In this case, we are considering blame, but you can do this for anger or shame, so think about the emotion and see where you feel it in your body.

Sense that this is not just a thought but a feeling you are holding within you. It may help you to focus on this feeling if you give that feeling a colour. What colour might that feeling be?

Now consider what emotion lies beneath this feeling. What is it? Fear? Loneliness? Anger?

Consider what emotion lies beneath the initial feeling, then as quickly as you can, look for the layer beneath that, trace the feelings down, one below the other, like peeling an onion. Keep following this process.

For example, what lies beneath fear, if that came up for you? Fear of what? Maybe beneath that, you might find isolation, lack of belonging. Keep searching down until you reach the bottom of the feelings.

It is your feeling. I am just giving you examples here of what might lie underneath, but we are all different. What is it for you?

Keep revealing the feelings beneath the feelings and eventually you will reach a point where there is nothing there, nowhere left to go. You have peeled back all those painful feelings and found the gap beneath them.

So, from this point, what happens? You have moved through all those negative emotions and found a void there. We can begin to come up now, once we have peeled back all those feelings, found the gap beneath, and we can begin a new chain.

Feeling something positive under there, relief at moving through all those bad feelings, finding the void beneath, which can then lead to peace, to calm, to a new sense of ease.

Exercise
Writing a letter

If you feel strong feelings of blame towards a parent, that will need to be released to process it. This is what I have achieved through the letter I wrote to my father, which is the opening chapter. I had always seen him as my dad and not an individual with his own journey and story. I saw his world circulating around me, this other child felt like a betrayal. I blamed him for letting me down.

By writing the letter, I was able to work through those emotions and I tried to understand what had happened to lead him to such a mistake, which is how I saw it.

I told him my disappointment and by doing so in the way that I did, it made some of the drama of my feelings dissipate.

If your parent is still alive, you may have the opportunity to discuss these feelings if you want to and they are receptive to listen. However, it is easier to really work out these feelings on paper first or even as an alternative. So, write a letter or dialogue to your parent, but add some reflection. How was this experience for them, what led them to it, how might it have felt for them? I would add here that the letter is for you to work through your feelings and it may not be wise to send it. It may help to have the support of a therapist to discuss whether you should take this further or not once it is written.

It is a tough point in the process of growing up, which can happen at any age, to face the fact that it is not all about you.

This situation you may find yourself in is probably hurting many people in your family story. It may be useful to consider the wider impact of this DNA event in this dialogue.

The ramifications can be very widely spread into different generations of the family and even family friends.

Writing things down can be very cathartic and as it takes time, it gives you the opportunity to really engage with what you think, going deeper than you might realise.

Chapter nine

EMOTIONAL STATES – SHAME

The most interesting writing about shame is found in the work of Brené Brown, particularly in her book *Daring Greatly*, though her other works touch upon it.

There is a whole range of types of shame we can experience, but we are looking at a very specific life event that can trigger shame, that of the person whose world view has changed through DNA revelations, so we will focus on that.

This type of shame relates to old recordings in our subconscious that reflect our culture or what we see as cultural norms. In this case, it is that of legitimacy versus illegitimacy, which surprisingly can still be used as a weapon against people today, and insults around legitimacy still pervade. According to Annette Kämmerer in her article on shame, this emotion comes when we feel we have transgressed the norm. This is in our situation and, therefore, is transferred shame.

Having perhaps lived a life relating to fitting into the cultural norm of family life and then finding yourself outside this may feel incredibly damaging to the sense of self and bring shame. This is a tough kind of shame to deal with, as it is essentially not yours. You did not do anything to earn it, but you are left carrying the impact of it.

Shame usually provides us with the opportunity to change and evolve our thinking to improve our processing, but as it is not a result of our own actions, it is more challenging to resolve. I have to say even in my position, though not the one immediately affected, I found myself seeing my father differently, therefore questioning the perception of my family life. I did feel some shame at my father's actions, actions that now put our family outside the view of expected social convention.

The guiding force of shame comes from fearing what others will think. It is not about what we think, so this involves a kind of mind reading and is based on assumptions, which is entirely unhelpful. We do not actually know if the family revelations we face will make people see us differently or treat us differently. I think when it is indirect shame, perhaps we sometimes fear the pity of others even more than direct judgement.

When shame kicks in, we are then a hostage to our limbic system, so we go into flight/fight/freeze or flop. When in this state, we are no longer using our thinking forebrain but have retreated into survival mode governed by the hindbrain. Being prepared to run and to fight is not helpful in this situation, we need to apply our thinking faculties rather than physical actions.

Brené Brown argues that shame is a fear of disconnection and this ties in with the work of Indra Torten Preiss in his work *Family Constellations*. Preiss argues that shame is a vital part of our survival instinct and avoiding doing anything that could cause shame helped us to remain a part of our tribe, and in man's early development, your chances of survival were always greater within the tribe.

For me, safety is then the key here. We feel unsafe if we are not connected to and accepted by others. If we do something shameful, we will no longer belong, and of course, someone who finds they are not necessarily in their genetic family may feel this fear of no longer belonging or being cast out. This may not be a conscious fear, but it is there nonetheless and it is then accompanied by the associated feelings of rejection.

Though it seems, in many cases, there appears to be a kind of instinctive knowing that something is different, that sense of belonging and the safety that comes with it is already challenged. It is important to tackle the feelings of shame because it can lead to higher rates of anxiety and depression, according to philosopher Hilge Landweer at the Free University of Berlin. It is argued that if you do not develop a strong sense of self in adolescence, then you may be more prone to feelings of shame, as shame also has links to the nervous system and the malfunctioning of that system. We, therefore, need to pursue some ways to navigate shame in a constructive way and at the same time enhance the sense of self.

If you have pursued some of the identity exercises, then you may have already done some work to combat shame as you are working on that sense of self.

One thing we can do is to move the subconscious into the 21st century and challenge those ideas of cultural norms that have changed significantly over the last couple of decades; look at the evidence for the changes of perception around family life.

In 2022, fifty-one per cent of children born in England and Wales were born to women who were not married or in civil partnerships. By the age of fourteen, forty-six per cent of children are not living with both parents. The map of what constitutes conventional family life has changed.

Also, we need to consider that it is not the role of a child to carry the shame and guilt of actions they had no part in.

We are responsible for our own actions; we cannot be responsible for those who have gone before us.

Exercise

To examine your role with shame here, we are going to use some of the elements of a technique that comes out of CBT, often called 'Socratic Questioning' after the Greek philosopher Socrates. There will be a series of questions, and I would like you to get a piece of paper and write down your responses.

I would like you to think about the shame you are feeling. Is there evidence that you have done something to be ashamed of in relation to your new family situation? Whatever your position is, what have you personally done, not anyone else?

What evidence do you have to justify your feelings of shame, and what evidence is there against them?

Is this feeling of shame based on facts, or are you basing this shame on feelings?

Is the way you are thinking about your new family situation what we might call black-and-white thinking? But the reality may be more complicated?

We need to examine the way you are responding to and interpreting people's actions in this situation; are you making any assumptions here about how people have acted or felt? What might their motivations have been? How do you think the adults involved might feel about the situation now?

Might other people on the outside of this situation be able to see an alternative view, interpret this differently?

Could your thoughts now about shame be an exaggeration of what is true?

Having completed this exercise, I would like you to put it to one side and repeat it in one year's time to see if your answers are different.

Exercise
Perceptual positioning

Instead of being you for a moment, we need to move out of the me-centre view and see beyond it.

I would like you to imagine that you can step into a time machine and travel back into the past. As the adult you are now, with the wisdom you have now, set the coordinates to the time your parents had to make a decision about what story to tell you, maybe both parents or one parent had to make a decision that was best for everyone concerned.

They may have discussed this with a friend. You are a time traveller, see what you can see, hear what you can hear. Observe them working through what they can do. Use your imagination to think this through in a detached way. You could imagine it is a film storyline and you are watching this unfold on the screen.

It may help this exercise to use a picture of one of your parents at the age they would have been to really focus on and go back and visit them. They were probably still very young, maybe younger than you are now.

What are their options right now? Your situation is unique; your parents might be married, married to others, very young. See what they had to consider at that time. Is there something they could have done differently? If so, how would that have affected your life? What would have been different? Would it have been all better, a bit better, or not better at all?

You are not the child in this situation; you are examining the role of the adults trying to decide. Write down what their options were. They may not have made the best decision. Imagine it is you now. Would you have done better? Perhaps you would, but you are in possession of hindsight. They did not have that luxury.

Remember, they did not know you would go ahead and test your DNA. They thought you would never know.

Could they have been trying to protect you? Whatever your role is in the story, the immediately affected person or a sibling, examine whether they were protecting themselves or, indeed, someone else. Observe and consider what is really going on here.

Is there anything going on here that you need to really be ashamed of? After all, they are making the decision now for you.

Exercise
NLP visualisation technique

I would like you to think about the feeling you wish to release, whether that be anger, blame, shame, resentment or any emotion that is linked to this experience which you feel is hurting you.

I would like you to visualise that emotion and give it a colour; if that emotion had a colour, what colour would that emotion be?

See it in your mind's eye, or if you are not very visual just think of the idea of a colour for that feeling, give that feeling a colour. For some people it is red, for you, it may be something different….what colour is it for you?

Think about that colour. If you can visualise that colour in your mind, see it as clearly as you can, just sitting with the idea of this colour.

Now we are going to put this colour into a shape, give that feeling a shape, I wonder what shape that feeling would be for you, could it be round? Square? A triangle, perhaps, or a sickle, perhaps? It could be a many-sided shape, the shape of an object, it can be any shape at all, it is your feeling, see that colour take a shape, or think about how that colour might take shape, see it form into the shape that you have chosen. Sit with this idea in your mind for a moment, the feeling has a shape and a colour now.

What we are going to do next is to give it a texture. What texture might this emotion have? Is it bumpy? Is it spiky? Is it scaly, perhaps, maybe bumpy and waxy like the surface of a lemon? What is the texture of the feeling; if it were to have a texture what would it be?

This feeling really has an identity now with its colour, shape and texture. The next thing we need to do is to give that feeling a sound.

If that feeling had a sound, what would the feeling sound like? Is it a loud drilling sound…or perhaps the tolling of a bell? Could it be a shrill, high note? Whatever feels the right sound for that feeling, give that feeling a sound.

That's right.

The next thing we are going to do to help process this now is to imagine a colour that makes you feel comfortable. This is going to be a healing colour, a colour that will help you manage this, a colour with a warm and comfortable feeling, a relaxing warm and comfortable feeling. Think about that colour. Visualise that colour if you can. Clearly, now, a different colour from the one we started with in this exercise, what would it be?

We will now bring the object you created that is associated with the bad feeling and surround it, surround that shape with the colour of the good feeling, surrounding the object, swallowing it up, wrapping it up like wrapping it into a blanket, surrounding it and changing it. As you do so, you will probably find, yes, you will probably find that the object changes colour, and if you go back to the sound, the sound has become at least quieter, or maybe it has changed altogether into a gentler sound, a more comforting sound, with the change of the colour and the sound, is the texture different. Is it smoother? Is it softer?

Dissolve and change the bad feeling as you change and alter your object.

The purpose of this exercise is to prevent the bad feelings from overwhelming you by creating the object. You are containing the feelings; they are no longer coursing through your whole being, but you have controlled and isolated them.

By then using the new colour like a blanket and surrounding and changing the object, you have taken action. You are not being passive. You are not a victim. You have taken control and neutralised what may have felt like an attack upon you. You have used your skill and ability to process the feeling and protect yourself.

Chapter ten

EMOTIONAL STATES – GRIEF AND LOSS

Grief is an emotion that is not limited to bereavement. It relates to loss of any kind and there is undoubtedly loss when you find you have a different parent to that which you thought, or a full sibling becomes a half-sibling, your partner has had a child you did not know about, or indeed your family make-up has changed in some way.

What had been your truth has been challenged. This then challenges your sense of who you are and may make the memories you have seem different, somehow less real. You may feel that certainty and security have been taken away from you; this is loss for which you are entitled to grieve.

No one can really take your memories away from you; they are your reality, but they can feel tarnished in some way.

As with a conventional bereavement, it is accompanied by a range of emotions, such as anger, denial and bargaining. Ultimately, the end of this process brings with it acceptance as we cannot change the past, we cannot change the family we were born into or any of those childhood experiences or later revelations about family. What we can do is change how we respond to the experience. Go to a position of non-resistance if acceptance feels too big a word. Resisting facts, resisting reality, gets us nowhere; embracing it leads to growth.

You may not be ready to reach that point of non-resistance, but ultimately, you really have no alternative in the end. It just depends on how long it takes you to get there.

The situation you are in is real and unalterable. Inevitable events and the actions of others are outside our area of control. What we can do is work at controlling our response to it.

Denial is often deemed the first stage of grief and loss. The shock leads to a kind of paralysis and numbness because the information is too much for the psyche to absorb. We can align this feeling to the freeze state in the fight/flight response. We cannot run from it or fight it, so we freeze and pretend it is not happening.

It was certainly my response when I first received the DNA result linking me to my half-sister. It could not be true because if it were, it upended everything I believed about my life and, of course, it was an even greater change for her.

When I saw a picture of her and saw the contours of my own face in hers, I still repeated again and again that it could not be true. As I have already stated, we had a second DNA test to be absolutely sure, and then we had to accept it was true and start on that journey towards acceptance.

Still now, after two years, I have moments when I just feel like surely this is a mistake, it cannot be true, and I know she has these moments too. It is not a rejection of our relationship, but the challenge it poses to everything we knew about our lives seems so huge we fall back into denial. It is so much easier to deny than to begin to face the loss of your life story as you saw it. This first stage of grieving is designed to help us survive the initial shock of loss and that is no different in any grief or loss situation.

Anger is often seen as the second stage of grief, but it is such a huge emotion in the process we are discussing that we will look at it in more detail separately. All these stages of grief are designed to protect us from facing the pain of loss head-on and that is why it is a process that unfolds. Sometimes, you may even feel more than one of these emotions in a day, sweeping back and forth, trying to find a place of safety.

Bargaining is the next stage of grief, and at first, I did not think it had a place in this area of loss, as it usually involves a kind of bargaining with God, whether believed in or not, to spare a loved one, or let it all be a dream and I will wake up and that person will still be by my side. I realised after some thought that there is an 'if only' feeling that accompanies the bargaining within grief.

My sister and I both had thoughts of *if only we had not had the test, we would not know, and everything would have stayed as it was*. This is undoubtedly a form of bargaining, but there is no going back, as there is no way to do so with other big loss events like death either. Things before seemed safe, familiar and unchallenging, and now we know we have to deal with vast changes. The genie is out of the DNA bottle, and we cannot put it back in. We each said to each other in the early days, 'No offence, I really like you, you are a gift in a way, but I still wish I did not know or have to deal with this'.

So, we did face this kind of bargaining and maybe you have too. If only someone had kept the secret. What a dichotomy. We blame them all for the secrets. Then we blame them for them coming out.

Bargaining and 'if only' moments most commonly accompany sudden deaths, those moments you are completely unprepared for. It is a way to manage shock. In my family, we found ourselves in shock too. We were grieving for our old lives and our old selves.

Next, we face depression in this grief process. Partly, I think this comes when all the emotional turmoil has exhausted our nervous system. It can no longer maintain the agitated fight or flight. Then the tension of the freeze position cannot be maintained forever either as its rigidity becomes painful, impossible to sustain, so we fall into 'flop', a part of our nervous system response when we play dead, which would be the action within the wider natural world. If we do that, nothing will harm us.

When some time has passed, and all the denial and the bargaining and the anger have failed to change any of our circumstances, sadness fills us. We are flat, with no energy left to fight this change in our life situation.

And so finally all that is left for us is acceptance or non-resistance; we are no longer resisting the reality that we face. We cannot go on resisting it, as we have evidence to prove to us it is true and continuing to try to resist it only leads to more pain and confusion, whatever the loss we face.

That does not mean there is no more pain. It means you know the reality of the situation. You have at least come to terms with that and you can begin to heal.

Eventually, perhaps you are not there yet, but we may find some glimmer of positivity in the situation, whether the discovery of new relatives or maybe understanding ourselves better.

It may, in the end, explain some of our responses to things, our behaviours, our interest in knowing more about our birth family, connections with new ancestors, even if we have lost some, we have gained others. Maybe there are some interesting stories in the new family and you can connect with them.

You may have lost, but you have also gained. If you wish to explore deeper, deeper into yourself as well as your family, you may find that. It can even help you to understand your parents' behaviour more. It may answer questions that had seemed unanswerable for years.

When you are ready, mine for the positive things that you can find in this situation once you have processed those big and powerful emotions.

Exercise
Metaphor visualisation – tree roots

This metaphor is designed to reconcile the idea of the new family and the old existing family. When I was reading Nevslin's *Impact of Identity*, I was struck by the fact that she was Jewish, growing up as a minority in the USSR, a place where individuality was frowned upon, yet her Jewishness made her different.

She found her place when moving to Israel, where she felt greater belonging, yet there were things she had experienced growing up in Russia that she missed. She had to blend the old with the new. She could still enjoy her borscht, thus blending the old and the new lives.

I feel this is what someone who finds they have a new heritage needs to do to keep what they love from the old and embrace the new, and this is how I developed this metaphor to help this process.

Interestingly, she has a section in her book using the image of roots in your family as important, not an uncommon theme, I had been using this metaphor in my work for some time but had recently adapted it to incorporate the idea of new family.

I would like you to imagine, visualise that you are walking through trees, tall trees stretching up towards the sky…..if you do not find it easy to visualise, just follow this idea in your mind….so you are following a path…you may hear twigs snap beneath your feet….or perhaps, perhaps the ground is soft, mulched down by old leaf fall….look up at the canopy of branches and of leaves around you….. the sunlight dappling down through those branches…..

See the colours around you….

There is the brown of the bark, mottled or ridged, gnarled wood…..and the green of the leaves of the trees……maybe there are ferns sprouting up from the base of the trees…..are the leaves rustling in a gentle breeze?…

Maybe the sounds can anchor you deeper into this idea…..the birds singing from the top of the trees….. can you see fungi clinging to the bark of the trees….in shades of creams, beiges and browns?….

Look around you and see what you can see…..hear what you can hear here amongst the trees… what about smell?…maybe you can smell the damp earth?…or the smell of the wood?….the leaves….perhaps you might want to lean forward and touch that rough bark… running your hand over it….using all your senses to bring you into this moment amongst the trees….a part of the forest for the moment.

Walking on and hearing the rustle of the leaves even more now as the wind blows through the branches…. the movement of the branches creating patterns with the shadows as the sunlight dapples down….feeling the movement and life of the trees….strong and deeply rooted…….supple and strong…..see the roots that spread out from the base of the tree….spreading…. reaching across the ground…..then disappearing down….deep …deep into the soil…..

Look for a specific tree…. a tree that draws you towards it…… I do not know what your tree looks like....an evergreen.....or deciduous tree...so many to choose from.......but head over towards a tree and notice the particular roots of this tree .....that anchor this tree in the ground and bring it nourishment from the depths of the soil......nitrates drawn up through the soil to sustain and support this tree....

Now sit down with your back against the tree....... leaning back against it..... supported by the tree and the earth beneath you. ......those roots are like your roots....... your roots that support you and nourish you......the family you grew up in........roots deep in your family that no matter what happens in day-to-day life....how far you drift...how far you travel....you are still attached...supported by them...they are a part of your world....your roots in the past....no one can take away or remove your past...it is yours...roots in the past...

You have the roots that lead into your friendships... that support you....your friends choose you...choose to be a part of your world and they support you too.... roots that anchor you......when times feel hard...you are strong because you have these powerful roots...these roots that have been growing and strengthening.... going deeper over the years.......

Now....now you have some new tender roots..... routes into a new family....that become roots for your.....family you did not know you were connected to........nurturing these new tender roots.....perhaps feeling the energy that you can draw up from the knowledge that they are there too......now a part of your root system......drawing from all these people in our life......past……….. present...future……drawing up from the people in your life and you support them too.......you are a part of their root system too....your own echo-system interconnected ...supporting each other.

The tree is strong...you are strong...feel that strength pulsing through you...life pulsing through you here and now....the sap is the life blood of that tree...it flows through it carrying nutrients just as the blood pulses through you.

Aware of your life energy, your strength, as you absorb the rays of sunlight as it touches your skin, nourishing you as it nourishes the tree....you are at one with it all...at peace...the world may be full of hustle, bustle, go, go, go but it does not affect you here.

You are peaceful at ease, drawing in your strength, feeling the support of your roots that anchor you, always there for you, you are not alone, you are a part of something vast, a vast network of roots that connects you, anchors you and nourishes you….you have not lost anything….you have gained new roots….extra strength that is around you and part of you.

This exercise helps to ground you in your present new self. You are recognising the roots from your childhood, the family you grew up in and no one can take that experience away from you. They are real, a genuine experience.

But now you have more than that family. You are gaining something extra rather than losing something. Those tender new shoots from your new connections need nurturing and care in a way those old roots do not, as they are well established.

It may not be possible for you to have a direct relationship with your new DNA family, but this does not mean that you are not connected to them. This is something else that cannot be taken from you; it is a fact.

If possible, you can learn about that family, your ancestry, that web going back into the past to add to your story. This is about the growth of your sense of self. Allow yourself to see this new situation as an expansion of your network.

To make this idea more real you could draw an image of the tree, then put in and label all the roots that ground you now. Each root could have a name associated with it, a family name. You may want to include a root called the ancestors, as they are part of your root system too.

This exercise is not just relevant to those who find a new parent, but new half-siblings too. These have now become a part of your root system, and if a full sibling has become a half-sibling, it does not take anything from you. They are still a part of your root system growing up. Everything is expanding and not contracting. We are moving away from loss with this exercise and embracing growth.

If you have found that you have new ancestors, it may help to come to terms with these new roots in your past ancestry and find out where they came from. There may be some cultural or regional differences that you can explore and see if they have meaning for you. Find books and music from the area they come from, or look at pictures and see if the scenery speaks to you. There are those who argue we can inherit memory from our ancestors, so it may be that you can find new meaning in some of the things that draw and attract you.

Exercise
World view

We are going to do a different version of perceptual positioning to that which we did before, to put your new experiences into perspective. It may feel huge to you right now, but over time, it will find its place in your story.

After all, what in your real day-to-day life has changed? Your home has not been taken from you, your job or role in society. Your children, if you have any, are still your children. In fact, your life is still your life; it is under your control. In all practical senses, you are safe, and your normal day-to-day life has not changed.

I would like you to see yourself as you are at home sitting in a familiar room. Perhaps you are a bit worried about your current situation, struggling with the idea of change.

I want you to really be in your body there, re-experiencing being in your home, sitting there dealing with whatever is going on for you and then step outside yourself and sit or stand on the opposite side of the room. Look at yourself, see your body language, see your facial expression, take it all in, just watch, be an observer of you.

Now move outside the house and look in through the window at you sitting there, watching where you sit, seeing you in the context of what you can see of the room, the whole space there and you within it. Now I want you to use the power of your mind to float up into the sky, looking down at your home from above, as if you had x-ray vision and could see down into the house from above, seeing where you are, but also anyone else in the house, whatever they are doing, others in the building and then spreading out your perspective seeing your whole street from above.

Now, just seeing the rooftops, aware that there is life going on in all those buildings down there, like looking down on an anthill, you know it is all going on in there, but you are floating above it all now, seeing your street. But you know that down there is you, you, feeling a little unsettled.

Next, you are going to go even higher, floating now above your whole town, seeing your village or town from above the whole space spread out beneath you, aware of all the people living their lives down there, but seeing it from on high, it stretches out further as your perception widens now, but you are down there. In that town is a street and in that street is a home and in that home is a room and in that room is you, dealing with your feelings.

Your lens widens now to take in the whole county or region you live in, seeing it stretch out, towns and countryside, see what you can see, stretching out down there and you know in that region is a town and the town has a street and a home and in a room in that home is you.

Then we expand even further and you are looking at the whole country, your country spread out beneath you as if you are in a plane looking down at it and you know that in that country is a region and that region has a town and then there is a street and a home, in that home is a room in which is you dealing with your feelings.

Then expand again to the whole continent, which is spreading out beneath you, seeing your continent and then we go even higher, even higher and see the world, that familiar image of the globe with the predominant stretches of blue and green, see that below you now, a planet rotating in the solar system and then we are up higher amidst the stars, a dot above the whole solar system looking down. On that planet is a continent, on the continent is a country, the country has a region with a town and a street and a home, with a room in which you sit.

I wonder how it feels now as we plan our return down through the solar system, back seeing the earth, your continent comes into view and then your country, your country is there and your region within, zoning down again to your region and then to the town or village, seeing it spread out before you and finding your street, looking for your street.

I wonder if you can see it yet and, drifting down to your house, outside the window again, looking in, looking into the window and then you are back in the room, looking over at the place where you sit and then sitting there looking out at the world again, it can feel different now, will you let it feel different now, I wonder?

We may have a feeling that our world is not what we thought it was and where we have ended up feels very different to our expectations. We may feel separated from members of our biological family, whether a parent or sibling, but we need to examine the wider context. It is as it is; the world still turns, and you still need to eat and sleep, work, and care for your family, and we need to find a way to explore this.

Chapter eleven

EMOTIONAL STATES – ANGER

Anger is part of our fight/flight survival response. It is the flip side to anxiety; anger gives us the fight part of this response, anxiety the flight part.

Anger has both physical and psychological components to it. We may get the physical symptoms we associate with anxiety, like trembling, agitation, sweating and a racing heart rate. The psychological component works with the physical one. Often, it is the result of feeling threatened in some way. We may also feel we have been treated unfairly and ruminate on the feelings of injustice, as explained in *Overcoming Situational and General Anger* by Deffenbacher and McKay. Anger also comes when we feel rejected, judged, embarrassed or ashamed. It is all about being hurt. This hurt is often stoked by overthinking way beyond the immediate experience. For some people, the angry response becomes the normal way to deal with difficulty in life, and they work hard to justify it rather than trying to manage it or heal the triggering life experiences.

When we feel closely connected to someone, whether a close friend, partner or family member, we release a hormone called oxytocin. When we trust them and feel comfortable with them, this enables us to be close to them, particularly in the case of physical intimacy.

When we are angry, the production of this hormone shuts down so that we are then able to fight to defend ourselves, even if it is against someone we love. Whilst experiencing this, all empathy and compassion need to be buried deep to enable survival in the fight. If you were in a real, tangible, dangerous situation, you could not afford to have any positive feelings towards your opponent, or it would put you at risk.

You may have had the experience of rowing with a partner whom you would normally fight to protect, but in the heat of the moment, they almost seem like a different person; in that moment, they have become the enemy. They almost seem unrecognisable; you cannot imagine that sense of closeness. This can only happen with this change in body chemistry.

This feeling may seem familiar if you are struggling to come to terms with a parent or loved one lying to you about the past or keeping secrets from you; it alters who they are to you, and the protective anger steps in. As it is tied into our survival, it can be very easily triggered if we feel threatened in any way.

When anger is in full state, it is hard to think clearly as blood flow is diverted away from your thinking forebrain into your survival hindbrain. To enable us to help manage the feelings of anger, we need to let the initial blast of it pass before we can look at healing it.

The first thing to consider here is that this is a natural response, and sometimes it may feel like your world has been turned upside down, your trust in your parent/parents has been broken, and most importantly, your sense of self has been threatened, that carefully constructed edifice that provides you with resilience to deal with life's challenges.

I would never say anger is a bad emotion. Some therapists say you must not feel angry, but this is, in my opinion, unrealistic. Anger is part of a process we need to go through as we face difficult situations in our lives. It thinks it is protecting us, resistance, so it will not help, but what I would say is it needs to be worked through and ultimately released.

Hanging on to anger will only hurt you in the long run; it is a short-term fix in the moment of discovery, but it cannot help you in the long term as it pushes people away. Anger creates rupture in your close personal relationships and healing comes with repair. It can erect a permanent barrier between you and your family, and you need to reach the point where you can begin to understand the decisions that were made long ago in the past when the current moment was not envisaged and we have already begun to consider this.

One of the first things you can do with your own anger is to begin to notice when it arrives. You might feel it arriving first in your body somewhere and feel that red mist creeping into your mind. Start to notice the very moment it begins and keep noticing; that will be the beginning of change for you.

After an expression of this anger, it is worth being aware of whether it has been directed at the person who triggered it in the first place or you have displaced this anger by directing it elsewhere because it may feel easier to do this than tackle the real problem.

This emotion is one of the five stages of grief, so it is a very likely companion, as is any situation related to loss.

Exercise
Observation

I would like you to sit down quietly for a moment and imagine you are an observer of this angry outburst, see yourself floating out of yourself as if you could hover above, or maybe like a fly on the wall observe this exchange of feelings. I wonder how it feels to watch yourself?

Can you detach yourself enough from the feelings to just be an observer for a moment? How do you look in that moment of anger? What is your facial expression?

How do you sound? What kind of words are you using? Are they really the kind of words that come naturally to you?

Now, I would like you to take this observation to another level. I would like you to float into the person you had been directing your anger towards. I wonder if you can do that? Imagine how they feel in that moment, what are they saying?

Be them in the moment and see how it feels.

This may be too difficult the first time you try it. Just observing yourself may be enough, but if you can take this next step, it will be helpful for you.

This is perceptual positioning again, and it helps you to get a greater perspective on the problem.

One thing we need to hold onto is that the people we are close to do not deliberately set out to hurt us. That does not mean they do not hurt us, but it may come out of protecting themselves or perhaps a misguided thought about how they may protect you. There is always another perspective and our greatest growth can come when we see this.

Anger is such a powerful emotion and as we have considered, it is trying to help and protect us, but often it hurts us too; rather like anxiety is trying to protect us, but often just ends up limiting us.

Learning to at least observe these powerful emotions will help you on the way to resolution.

Exercise
Metaphor visualisation – fire

We are going to use a metaphor here in a visualisation process to help you with your anger.

Now, we are not talking about resisting the anger that you feel. We are not fighting it in any way; we accept it is there, you feel it, and your feelings are valid. But I want to look at an idea to help you manage the anger. To do this, we are going to think about the idea of a fire.

A fire starts from a spark, a small spark that has to be fanned and encouraged to survive.

I wonder if you have ever seen fire started in the old-fashioned way by rubbing two sticks together, having one flat piece of wood or stick upon the ground and then taking a slim spindle-like stick, holding a stick between the palms of the hands, pressing it down against the other piece of wood, and spinning it, twizzling and spinning, pressing down into it, again and again, you have to put quite a lot of effort into powering the twig between your hands, rubbing and spinning the spindle twig and then you are rewarded by the smoke rising from the base from the friction of the rubbing of the wood.

If you have never seen this or done it, use the power of your mind to imagine it. Then, there is the spark, finally, a spark appears, which you blow upon to sustain it, then you need to feed it with materials that will burn, some wood shavings or some wool, and it will burst into fire, a flame will shimmer before you, real fire not just a spark any more.

But you have to keep fanning the flames, encouraging them, and you have to keep feeding the fire to keep it alight. It requires more and more to sustain it and make it grow bigger and bigger. It needs oxygen to survive. So many things in place to keep the fire burning. Even if this is a new idea to you, but you have seen someone make up a fire in a grate, it cannot be abandoned; it needs care to sustain it, and it too needs more and more fuel to keep it going.

I would like to suggest to you that your anger is just like that fire, starting from a spark, those deep feelings, all enmeshed together, a flare of anger, up it rises and bursts out as you think about your situation, as you think about how it makes you feel, all those emotions we have discussed bubbling away to provide more and more fuel to sustain it.

You do have to work at it just like the fire to sustain that anger, to keep it there, it is tiring, draining, exhausting, running over the feelings, the thoughts, justifications, going around and around in your mind.

Fanning it with your attention, feeding it with new reasons, new ideas of why it is justified, why you have a right to feel it, justifying your anger to yourself, feeding it and making it flare. Of course, you have the choice to remove your attention from it and stop fanning the flames, stop nursing that anger into life, stop feeding that anger to make it stronger.

I wonder if you can catch it when it is just a spark, just beginning. When that thought pops into your mind, you know the one, the one that triggers it, the one that you roll over and over in your mind. Can you catch it when it begins and pause for a moment? Just hit the pause button and look for another thought. If the anger is focused on a person, can we think perhaps of something they got right instead of wrong for a moment? Just give it a chance. Look at the balance sheet here.

We are not saying what has happened is not wrong or not hurting you, but is there one small thing in your life right now that does still feel ok, good, perhaps a friendship or a relationship? Can we focus on that instead, just for a moment? Can we catch this spark before it has truly caught fire? Can you stop the anger or pause it before you withdraw your attention from it and it fizzles out?

I wonder if you have noticed when you have left that anger behind, times in the past perhaps around other things, when you have known it, the anger, that powerful wild emotion, in the past, how you cannot reignite it, in fact sometimes it is hard to remember just how you managed to create such a massive fire from such a small spark, in the past, that was then of course, before this now.

Will it always feel like this, I wonder, is that possible?

Will you be snuffing it out? You could even imagine, more than withdrawing your attention and no longer fanning the flames of it. You could see yourself throwing a bucket of water over it and completely snuffing it out, the best way to be sure, to be sure of leaving it in the past where it belongs.

I wonder when you will notice that moment has passed. Right away? Or will you notice the fire has gone out a few minutes from now?

It may take some time, it took me some time, but we have time. We can abandon the fire and leave it to its own devices, let it fizzle out. Even without the bucket of water, the fire in the grate, untended with no more fuel, will become glowing embers, just ash and dust. It will be such a relief as we feel the raging fire begin to go down, to flicker and fade, the embers aglow, then the last glow disappears, a little smoke rises and then, then it is ash and dust and we feel the relief from it, now the healing can begin.

Exercise
Cartesian questions

This therapeutic approach is drawn from Neuro-Linguistic Programming. It is often used as part of what is called an ecology check to check the need for change.

In this, we ask four key questions. I am going to base it around one of the emotions we have covered, but you can apply it to any of them. I will provide answers to the questions so you can see how it works, but then answer the questions for yourself and see what comes through for you.

What will happen if you *do* let go of your anger? Potential answer: *I will feel more peaceful, calmer and more at ease.*

What will *not* happen if you let go of your anger? Potential answer: I will no longer be trapped by actions from the past.

What will happen if you do *not* let go of your anger? Potential answer: I will continue to feel upset and distressed, caught in repetitive thoughts, ruminating on my pain.

What will *not* happen if you do *not* let go of your anger? I will stay distressed, I will continue to provoke my pain and loss, I will remain trapped, unable to move forward.

From all this questioning, you can make a decision. You can decide to stay with that feeling and do nothing to challenge it, leave yourself trapped in the emotion, or you can make a commitment to make the change, begin to challenge those thoughts and begin to process the emotions, leading you to a place ultimately of acceptance.

You are making some active choices here. Although it may seem passive to stay the same and not change, it is still a choice. You can choose to stay angry, or you can choose to break free.

You may not be ready yet to let go of blame, shame, anger or any of the thoughts and feelings we have discussed, but it takes huge energy to maintain all this pain. In the end, you will run out of the energy to fuel it, and it will wind down in time, so why not try this sooner and spare yourself as much time in pain?

Chapter twelve

EMOTIONAL STATES – BELONGING

Belonging is a powerful driving force within us. It is innate, a primary need, as it keeps us safe. If we belong to a group, our survival prospects are greater. This takes us back to a time when we lived in a tribal culture where real and practical dangers from predators surrounded us. We also had to strive for enough food to eat and find the security of shelter. If we felt ill, we would have needed someone to tend to us until we could fend for ourselves again. Thus, we needed to belong to a tribal group.

Belonging forms part of our emotional development and can, therefore, impact how we go on to interact with society. Our future employment opportunities and access to further education can be impacted by our sense of belonging in our developmental years. We learn early on that social acceptance is the root to belonging. We may feel that if we find that we are not the person we thought we were genetically, we will no longer be socially acceptable. Much of this is, of course, perception rather than based on fact.

Survival of the lone wolf is infinitely riskier. Even a tree's chances of survival are compromised if they are planted alone rather than part of a wood.

Brené Brown defines belonging as being the innate need to belong to something that is ultimately bigger than us. This state of belonging is challenged when we feel we may not belong in the family we grew up in, as our parentage has changed. With the tree roots metaphor that you have already encountered, I am trying to show that you are expanding the groups you belong to rather than them contracting, as no one can steal your past from you or to where you belonged then.

The Springtide Institute has a simple phrase to sum up belonging: I am noticed, I am named, I am known. Their research into loneliness and depression in adolescents found these topics coming up again and again, providing them with the basis of how we can support people who feel isolated and not belonging. These concepts bring us back to our thoughts on identity: to be noticed as an individual and to be known, for me, means to be understood for who you are. In my work as a therapist, I feel my first job is to help individuals feel they are understood. By being understood, they are seen, and they feel valid. They are no longer alone.

Sometimes, belonging can be damaging as it can lead people to do things that are not in their nature, such as physically hurting another person or joining the class bully to taunt another who is weaker or perhaps a bit different, just to remain within the group and not risk being the outsider. So, like many things, it is a double-edged sword. This is described in a paper called *A Need to Belong*, which describes it as a need to create a sense of belonging by othering people in different social groups.

To genuinely belong, we should not have to alter ourselves or try to make ourselves fit in and be accepted; that is not real belonging and can only ultimately be painful, as deep down, we cannot kid ourselves. We know we do not fit. It is hard to maintain such an act of contortion of the self to keep in the belonging state. Also, we know it is fake, so we remain feeling at risk, unsafe, in fact, the opposite of belonging.

So, find where you do fit. Do not try to contort yourself into something you are not. Remember the work on your identity? Be true to who you are, and you will find where you really belong. It may be your sense of belonging has been challenged all your life as you feel you did not seem like your siblings or you felt so different to a parent. If a DNA test has revealed to you why this is, it can help you make sense of those feelings of not belonging or feeling different. This is an opportunity to find your true belonging, to stop trying to fit in and really belong.

Brené Brown argues that to belong, we need to be accepted for who we are. Being inauthentic all the time is a waste of our inner resources. It is like swimming against the current, not in the time to flow with the current of who you are, and enjoying getting to know who that is and finding where you truly feel yourself. This can be quite a journey, but the results are worth it.

Exercise

The metaphor below is designed to help you understand that you can fit into a new group or family without entirely abandoning where you came from. Your mind can interpret it in whatever way you wish, whether linking you more to your biological family or to the original family; the link is there both ways.

Sycamore seed visualisation

I wonder if you are familiar with a sycamore tree? They have these amazing seeds that look rather like a boomerang. I wonder if you have ever seen a sycamore seed fall? It twists and turns, spinning like helicopter blades around and around until it reaches its destination, spinning like a top in the breeze, off it travels to start a new life.

I would like you to imagine this in your mind's eye, that creative part of you, it is a day in the woods, a wood full of sycamore trees, and it is just the right time of year for them to release their seeds, to create new life in the forest.

I would like you to imagine the sound of the fluttering leaves and maybe some birdsong emanating from the tops of the trees. Perhaps you can smell the damp earth or the rich woody smell of the bark of the trees, really anchor yourself in this image. Sunlight dapples through those branches as they sway in a gentle breeze.

As you watch this scene before you, a plump ginger cat is stalking through the trees on his own adventure, exploring, listening and looking, perhaps chasing a flicker of movement in the trees, a shimmer of movement at the edge of his vision.

So pre-occupied is he with his quest, his chase, that he does not notice the sycamore seed that is spinning down through the air towards him, that twisting and turning, taking this new hope of life on its journey, the cat does not know that it will be contributing to the new life of a tree, changing its whole destiny, as that seed lands on the back of the plump cat, the cat takes off at a bound and dashes through the trees, chasing a small bird, yet unknowingly carrying the seed with him as he races along, until a low branch rubs against the fur on the back of the ginger cat.

Eventually, the seed is dislodged at last, quite a way from where its journey began, and lands on the damp earth, and slowly, imperceptibly slowly, that seed becomes trodden down into the ground, pushed into the soil to begin the new life of the forest, a new tree, not quite where it may have expected to be, but it has found its place in the forest.

The rain comes down and the sun shines and all the conditions are right, so the seed grows, shoots of life burst through the surface of the soil and then it is a small sapling and it continues to grow, it grows and it grows into a strong and rooted tree, a tree that is a healthy sycamore, the product of that sycamore from far away. The originating tree and the new sapling that evolves and grows are eternally connected, they share a beginning and a belonging.

Nothing and no one can take this connection away. It is there, fixed, a given. The new tree may not be aware of its origins, but it does not matter, the tree can still be strong and healthy. This sycamore is in such healthy soil, it has the right amount of sunlight and nutrients up through its young and healthy roots that are pushing through the soil.

It can take advantage of where the seed had landed, not a cramped wood jostling for space, for healthy soil and enough sunlight, this seed landed well, in just the right spot for this tree to grow, and it has deep roots now, roots of its own, grounding strong roots that anchor it and make it powerful, contributing to the community of the forest. It can stand tall and strong and proud as it grows and flourishes.

It is part of the forest, part of the whole, but a strong individual tree, sometimes we think they all look the same, but each tree is different, each tree has something to offer to the forest, that great ecosystem of life.

The trees all support each other, they have methods of communication, and they support each other through their root system. If one is weak, they will feed each other through the roots, until the tree becomes strong again. Even trees need community, the lone tree does not thrive as the tree in the forest does.

It does not question where it belongs, so long as it is a part of the whole forest, that ensures survival, it ensures growth. These vital trees create the oxygen we breathe, all playing their part, all from that one tiny seed spinning on the breeze and carried afar by the ginger cat to its new beginning a place where it can grow and develop into a healthy tree.

You know what I am saying here, through the story of the seed. You may not be with your biological parents, or maybe just one of them, but you are still connected to your origins, you have found a place to grow and develop into the person you are, an individual with strengths and abilities, contributing to your community, whether the family you grew up in, a family you have created or the wider community.

You have your place, you do belong, where the seed originated is only a small part of the story, what you have become, who you are is what is important, we have considered all that contributes to your identity, you are so much more than your biological origins, fate has dictated by whatever range of circumstances that you did not have a life with both your birth parents but that is not your whole story, is it?

There is so much more to you than that.

If instead of being displaced yourself, your experience has been that you have discovered a full sibling is only a half-sibling, you can still celebrate the life you have shared together in your piece of the forest and be glad that this seed pitched up near you.

If you have discovered you have a sibling outside your family, then remember the link is there, always there, to where the story began. It is a simple metaphor, but allow it to help you gain perspective on your situation. Let it connect with and speak to you to help you with your situation.

Maybe, at this point, it is worth examining where you really want to belong. This ties in with the work on your core values we examined earlier.

Consider whether this change affects you any wider than your family situation, and take a reality check on how much it has altered your real place in the world.

If you feel rejected, do you really want to belong to that person or group of persons? This is an opportunity to really examine where you want to be rather than stumbling blindly into your place in society.

We are no longer living in a world where not belonging to a social group or family group will threaten our physical survival. That is what your sense of belonging is for, as we have discussed. You will survive. You are not in real practical danger; you are in a position of perceived danger, and you can negotiate your way out of this position by making some new and active choices for yourself.

Chapter thirteen

INTEGRATING THE PAST – MEETING IN THE SUBCONSCIOUS

When I was in my twenties, I read a book that had a huge impact on me called *One* by Richard Bach. In this book, the author pursued the many paths that his life might have taken if he had made different choices at key decision points or even if chance had a different path in store for him.

He details in his book how he narrowly missed being one of the pilots who dropped the atomic bomb over Japan in 1945. How different he would have felt if that had been his path. He met the love of his life in a lift and enjoyed a good life partnership. What if he had been five minutes later and they had never met?

I found this concept fascinating, and I feel it has a role to play now in building my relationship with my sister. What if we had met sooner? What if?

In my book *The Trauma Effect,* I use a version of timeline therapy, which I have called an ancestral timeline, to meet a significant part of my family who died before I was born. I experienced this in a light trance, and it was a very powerful experience.

The mind does not differentiate between fact and fiction, which is why it is so important to be cautious around the thoughts that we entertain.

That is why a dream or nightmare can seem so very real when we awaken. We have, for all intents and purposes, had that experience, whatever it might be. It explains the power over us of a film, novel or even a game that can take us on a rollercoaster of emotion.

I have cited many sources in my books to evidence that what we imagine in our minds is a real and actual experience. Thus, many of the exercises I suggest have such power, I am going to cite another one here to explain the following exercise more clearly.

In 1995, Pascual Leone put together a research group of people who had never played the piano. He put them into three groups: one just stared at the piano, one did simple finger exercises, and one group imagined themselves playing the piano. They all had brain scans before and after five days had passed. The scans showed changes in enhanced brain activity. The most significant surprise was that those who were imagining playing had the same brain activity as those who were actually practising. Our brains, therefore, do not differentiate between the two experiences.

This is why athletes can improve their performance by imagining excelling in their sport. It reminds me of my early fascination with Descartes' words: *I think, therefore I am*. I feel this means *how I think dictates who I am and what I am capable of doing*.

With this in mind, I wanted to integrate my sister into my past. I had some photographs my sister had given me, which in our early days together, we compared with such fascination as we looked for traces of each other within them.

I used some of these as a focus for this journey and wrote some ideas that were then presented to me in trance. The work I did follows. This may help you to do some integration work of your own, or perhaps it is an idea you can discuss with a therapist.

This is a story of what could have been!

Let's introduce him first, our dad. He has short, jet-black hair, neat into the neck at the back but with a curl at the front that sometimes flops into his eyes. 'Rakish', they would have said years ago. His eyes are green, a khaki green with golden flecks, and his skin sallow. He has that hint of a smile on his lips and that quirky raised eyebrow, which I wonder now if he perfected in the mirror, as it is so magnetic. He is slim, not too tall, about 5 ft 8. He is wearing a black polo-neck sweater, which was all the rage back then. That is how I see him now in this special moment.

And what about me? I am seven years old. I am in that dreadful purple polka-dot dress that came out for special occasions. I would be much happier in my jeans. I have those same green eyes and a square jaw, which are a little less defined at this age, but there nonetheless. I have long, brown hair tumbling about my face, and I look rather happy in myself; a slight smile also plays upon my lips. I am full of childish anticipation, not really understanding the magnitude of the situation, its complexities and ramifications.

I am about to meet my new sister, but my mother is not her mother. I cannot quite figure this out. My mother is not thrilled at all about this meeting but determined I will show up neat and tidy in my dress, giving a good impression to this other mother. We are in a house I do not know, and the adults are standing awkwardly around. My father places the small bundle into my arms. I am not interested in the tensions in the room, though even I can feel them; it feels confusing.

I am here for this, to meet this tiny creature, this bundle in my arms. Her hair is so fair. That is a surprise, and it is so full of curls, tight little curls wound around her head. I remember seeing a picture of Dad like this.

She gazes up at me with an intensity that surprises me too. She has darker eyes than mine, but still, they are green, more a plush green of the forest. Her arm comes up, waving in my face, and I grasp it, then letting her tiny hand wrap around my forefinger, I smile and look up. I gaze around the room, a broad grin on my face, but no one else seems to be smiling. Even Dad has lost that quirky twitch of his upper lip.

How can they all be so stiff and unyielding with this cute baby in the room?

I find a chair and sit down and treasure this first moment of connection between us, and in this moment I know I would fight dragons for her, that I will protect her come thick or thin. Ignoring the scowl on my mother's face, I hold this infant and begin to tell her things about the world that I think she should know. She should try rhubarb and custard sweets first, and when she is old enough to try it, there is something I do with Coca-Cola and vanilla ice cream that I know she will love. I wonder if she will be interested in my toy cars; maybe not. She can have the Pippa doll that I was given. I never really play with that.

I see a little boy of around three, peering from behind the other mother's legs, looking over shyly. So is he my brother, too? No one mentioned a brother, just this baby sister. He stays back, peeping out from time to time. He has darker hair, his eyes deep, dark brown like the other mother.

Mum is hovering in the doorway as if she really does not want to be part of the scene, but something is preventing her from retreating, a rapt fascination on her face as she looks at the tableaux before her. Dad is near me, the other mother is on the other side of the room now, and the adults are all still standing while I sit on the sofa, prattling away to my little sister. The Pippa doll has some outfits. I tell her that I don't mind if she has them too. I just would rather not part with my Ford Capri dinky toy. Is that selfish? Well, there are limits to what I am prepared to share. I have to share my dad now, after all.

Though how much will I have to share him? Will she be living with us or with the other mother? No one tells me anything, though I hear them sometimes when they think I am asleep. How could I not as their voices rise in anger? But I still do not really understand.

In time, I do, at least a little. She stays with the other mother, and we roll forward in time. I become a teenager, we are back in London now and I hate it. I think it is to be nearer my little sister because for those first few years, we were hundreds of miles apart and met rarely. Dad had those regular trips to London, and I guess it was to see her, though I was told he was going up on business. I think they think I am stupid. I was rarely invited to go after that first meeting. I think Mum had put her foot down, or so it seemed. I did give her my Pippa doll, though.

She is around seven now and it is a special time. She is coming to stay for the very first time, just Dad and me in the cottage by the sea. He is picking her up from the other mother after lunch on a Saturday. Mum has gone over to Ireland for the weekend to visit her aunt, keeping out of the way, I think.

I am a bit nervous. I am 15. I have dyed my hair auburn, and it is shorter than before. I am in charge of what I wear this time, so I am in my jeans, a white t-shirt and one of my favourite things at the moment, a turquoise-coloured waistcoat!

I have been wondering what to do with her when she arrives. I thought a tea party with little cups and saucers on the beach might be fun. They arrive and my eyes well up. She is clutching the Pippa doll that is very much worse for wear now. She eyes me shyly and looks for approval. I give her a smile and go in for a hug.

Her hair is long and fair, and she has a lovely smile that seems to split her face in two. *Reminds me of Dad,* I think, and it lights up the room. I gaze at her and think she looks a bit like me in the polka-dot dress phase.

I tell her about the tea party on the beach and she nods in agreement, so off we set, leaving Dad behind to plan our dinner. I had packed a bag with all we needed. We make our way down the hill. I lay a blanket down and get all the mini tea things out and we make space for Pippa too. With great ceremony, we eat cake and actually drink juice from our cups and I try to ask questions to get to know what she likes to do. This is so new for me to be alone with her. I wanted to give her my Coca-Cola and ice cream thing that I promised her all those years ago, but Dad was afraid it would make her sick.

We walk down to the water, her little hand in mine, and paddle in the sea. It feels easy, that is a surprise, I want to tell the people around us that this is my little sister I am holding by the hand. *So what?* they might think. *Big deal.* Well, actually, it is for me.

When I feel she is growing tired, we head back up the hill and dinner is nearly ready. Dad is all flustered as cooking for his two girls is something new for him. When we sit down at the table, he does that thing that really winds me up when he does it to me. He asks her a stupid question that is way beyond her years about some country. Even I have no idea where it is. I tell him off, seeing her twisting uncomfortably in her chair and then it dawns on me how nervous he is and I try to get him to talk age appropriately, or as best as I know how to do.

Before we know it, bedtime arrives. I have been preparing for this as I want to read her a story. I don't know what she reads at home, but I loved the Mrs Pepperpot stories when I was her age and I still have the book, so she settled down to listen to that. I did not want Dad reading her those scary stories about outer space that used to fuel my nightmares when I was ten.

As I read, her eyes began to droop, then they fluttered and dropped closed. A big day for her too; a brave girl she had been to come and stay with us, and as she slept, I saw that the Pippa doll was tucked beneath her arm, and my eyes, they welled up again.

Time moves on. She is now the one who is fifteen and has a new boyfriend that the other mother and both fathers are rather worried about.

Now, this is a big sis thing. I can talk to him. I am in my post-university goth phase. Black, crimped, abundant long hair and all the requisite goth clothing paraphernalia.

I am going to check him out, so I knock on his door. I am diminutive in size, so I could be seen as no threat to anyone, but I muster all the presence that I will later use as a CEO to intimidate the chair of the board, leaving him all atremble. With the goth attire as an addition here, it has the desired effect. He is very wary, and I warn him if he does anything to hurt my little sis, he will not just have me to answer to but some of my goth mates, and he really does not want to meet my goth mates. Indeed, he clearly decides he does not, as he goes on to behave as good as gold to my little sis. He was also warned not to let her know that I had been around. He nodded his agreement whilst hastily shutting the door.

Now, we are both adults and my sister is working with my father in the office. He is teaching her about accounts, and they share an understanding and a passion for unravelling numbers, a gene that has passed me by, though I do my best to muddle through. They missed so much time from childhood that it is good they have this time to share as adults, getting to know each other.

On this day, I am meeting them at the office, and we are heading out to lunch, we three. Now, the love of food is a gene we all share or is that cultural, I wonder?

Without even asking, I know we will have all examined the restaurant menu in advance and pondered with pleasure what we will eat, and already know what we will choose, but will make a show of perusing the menu when the time comes to make that all-important order. Dad is in a well-cut suit these days, hair grey now and cut very short to keep that errant curl at bay. My sister's hair is long and fair with curls at the side, which mine also has if not cut short.

Mine is very short these days and I am in my dyed blond phase. I am working at *News International*, which has a strict dress code, so I am in a skirt suit – khaki green to match my eyes – with accompanying black high heels, briefcase in hand as I am heading on to a meeting in Chelsea after my allotted two-hour break.

My sister is in a light summer dress, and our father looks so proud to be going out with his two girls on his arm. They have something exciting to tell me, they say, but it must wait until we are sitting down.

So, with the re-examination of the menus complete, orders in and a nice bottle of Provençale rosé on its way, 'What is the story?' I say. It turns out that someone came into the office that day who recognised Dad's last name. She asked if he was any relation to Eugene Thomelin. 'Yes,' he replied. 'He was my father.' She went on to tell them that she was one of the spies Eugene had recruited to be dropped over France during the war and work with the French resistance. She was one of the few who survived long enough to come home. She had lots of praise for our grandfather, calling him a true gentleman, and Dad was so excited to meet someone who had known him back then.

Neither I nor my sister had ever known our grandfather as he died before we were born, and this unites us, the hunger for stories of him. She, too, was so excited to have been party to this story and this inside view of a man she never knew.

We went on to mine Dad for stories of those times, such as flying back to Normandy with his father just after the liberation of France, and as a fifteen-year-old boy, being greeted by the town band, his father given a hero's welcome, then watching the punishment of the collaborators with a fascinated horror and then finally reunited with the family there.

We feel blessed to have this shared time with our father and to, in some voyeuristic way, engage with our grandfather. A sense of belonging, there is that word again. Belonging to these people, learning their stories and knowing we are an extension of them.

Decades have passed. I cannot even call myself middle-aged anymore, as I am past my fiftieth year. My sister has given Dad two grandchildren on whom he dotes. He refrains from boasting about how one looks so like him, but the boys are infinitely patient with him, even though he trembles.

I had to call her today to say he had gone, one of the toughest calls of my life. He had battled Parkinson's for so long now he seemed indestructible. He was in hospital with an infection, and they told us we would be able to take him home soon and then things all changed. He had days left and was discharged to a nursing home.

I called with daily updates when I cycled along to the home. I put her on speakerphone so she could talk to him. I don't know if he could hear either of us by that time, but it helped me to have her there, even if only at the end of the phone. We had planned a visit for the following day, but I just had to phone to say we had left it too long. He was gone.

I saw him go. There one minute, then no more. His strong presence just left the room, leaving it bare. I leave Mum with him and hear her despair. So final, so complete this loss.

She will come to the funeral. I am determined of that; will I be able to meet her eyes as I speak my eulogy? He said he did not want one. He felt unworthy with all his talk of sin.

And the moment comes, we have a French flag and an EU flag on the coffin, still a bit controversial, but he loved being controversial in life, so why not in death? It is Bastille Day, so apt.

We meet at the entrance to the church, my sister and I. She has not seen so many of the people in his life before. It must be an overwhelming day.

A full Catholic mass is unfamiliar to me, but my sister has had her confirmation. She knows when to stand and sit and sink to her knees. I copy her.

Then it is my turn to speak. So many people have told me stories of him in the last few days, what he meant to them. Condolences have come from all over the world, and I share this. I say I do not need to tell him of the gentle man he was as everyone there knew him. I read from *Gitanjale* by Tagore, the last words I was saying to him, and then I bid my farewell in French. At that point, our eyes meet across the church and that is when I break.

Beloved husband and father of two, not one, but two.

We never got to share any of these things, but we have shared them now! Incidentally, the spy did drop into the office, though only Dad was there, but I thought it was a memory that we would have loved to share.

Chapter fourteen

FAMILY CONSTELLATION OR SYSTEMIC THERAPY

I have been intrigued for some time by Family Constellation Therapy, sometimes known as 'Systemic Therapy'. It was developed by psychotherapist Bert Hellinger and is underpinned by some main concepts which I will outline to fully understand how it can help in complex family situations.

To understand this, we first must acknowledge the work of Dr Bowen in the 1950s, who propounded the idea that families are not a random selection of individuals but that they form a unit. This unit is governed by an individual system that each has to work within. Families can be so different in the way the system operates; it is an emotional system, and we take this learning from the system into how we behave in our future relationships.

We are a small part of a system that is built up over many generations. This can make our future family life difficult, as our partner may have come from a very different system.

We need to understand that this means that whatever affects one member of the family affects everyone in that unit and that anxiety can move from one to another within that unit.

What you are experiencing now with the change in understanding your biological family will be affecting your family unit.

It also needs to be understood that the fusion of family members can happen within the family unit; the self is lost to the group. This means emotions and anxiety flow more easily between them. We could consider what happens when that fused state is challenged and an individual feels their place in the unit is affected. If they feel they are fused with someone who was not perhaps their parent after all, this will lead to a great sense of rupture within the relationship and other relationships within the family.

This also ties in with the map of reality idea that comes from NLP. Our family gives us a map, a system, a way of operating and we believe it without question. This is another way of understanding the system of the family using the map as a metaphor. The map is not the terrain, it is not reality but a version of it, as viewed by your family, as represented in your family system.

Bowen argues we need a strong sense of self, and this will be affected by our system. We have examined the importance of identity, which can clearly be affected by the system too.

Hellinger's therapeutic work is to take this understanding of the family system and look at ways of healing difficulties arising from the specific and unique system.

We have considered that we all need to belong. Belonging is, of course, vital to our survival, and we seek it within our primary bonding experience, our family and then the wider social arena.

Following on from this, we need to feel secure. Security comes first from belonging, but there needs to be a sense of social order within the family. Where do you sit between your parents and other siblings? What is your role within the family?

Bowen looks at the different roles in families of siblings, and he sees that gender and your place within the family will affect the characteristics you develop.

I read with some interest the definitions for female-only children compared to older sister with a younger sister and was fascinated to discover that I had little in common with the female-only child characteristics and ticked all the boxes of the older sister role.

Given I have only had this role in reality for two years now, I wondered about this. If in some way I knew I had a younger sister, though not consciously, whether through overheard conversations as a child that I did not fully understand at the time or a more esoteric interpretation, which could be that we instinctively know such things. I certainly recognised my sister from the moment I saw her, and the bond felt real. I was not meeting a stranger. Though it may be fanciful to imagine that I took on the role of older sister when my little sister was just a living ghost within our family, unacknowledged and forging her way elsewhere.

In Roberta Gilbert's book on the *Eight Concepts of Bowen Theory*, she outlines that we have a basic self, our core self and a pseudo-self. It is the pseudo-self that arises from our relationships within the family system. It is less thoughtful, more reactive and automatic. It is full of those learnings, the map of reality and not the essential self.

The basic self is the best of us and is objective. It bases its views on facts rather than feelings and needs good boundaries. It is the pseudo-self that will feel it is under attack when the family system feels compromised or challenged. Therefore, we need to hang onto and protect it even more than the basic self and draw upon it to feel safe amidst all the changes that may be faced.

A sense of family structure is needed that feels secure. If it is not there it can lead to problems developing in later life. Due to the issue of secrecy and lies we have already discussed, there could be some undercurrents affecting this sense of social order which leads to a feeling of insecurity. We need to feel a sense of equilibrium; again, this brings safety. If there is the constant shifting and changing of dynamics, changeable behaviours, or no sense of negotiation within the family, a sense of fairness in the distribution of affection, for example, will affect equilibrium.

If this is dysregulated in early life, then, again, it leads to later problems. In a family where you are unknowingly not the child of both parents and/or one parent has a secret family, we can imagine this family system will be under considerable strain.

In Family Constellation Therapy, they consider the importance of the role of the ancestors, which Bowen also did. Both modalities argue that the actions of the dead may still be influencing your world now. We see this clearly with inherited trauma, for example. You may now be feeling your sense of who those ancestors are is being challenged, or you may not even know who they are. Your whole context may be feeling askew right now.

This therapeutic approach can be practised in two different ways to examine and integrate the family system. Either a group of people gather and take on the roles or represent members within the family system, and the facilitator will direct them whilst the enquirer watches.

The participants will be positioned facing away or towards each other, which is very significant for the process, and they will be asked how they feel in that position, what is going on for them. They will be put in position by the enquirer or, in some cases, the facilitator. There will be a key question that the enquirer has brought to the session and feelings related to this will be worked through with intuitive questioning and guidance by the facilitator.

Another way this can be done is to use counters or even pieces of paper to represent members of the system. It is argued that each family has an energy field, which is influenced by all the events that have affected the family over the generations. We are affected by the field even though this is unconscious, so we are not aware of it. Working to understand the family system that creates this energy field will lead to healing.

An example cited in Joy Manné's book *Family Constellations: A Practical Guide to Uncovering the Origins of Family Conflict* has just three representatives to work through a particular constellation: one representing the enquirer, one her dead brother and one her new partner. Through the session, the enquirer is able to release her grief for her brother and begin to focus fully on her partner. This work is not passive, and it requires a desire and commitment to learn from what is revealed through the constellation work and to essentially self-actualise the change.

What is very interesting about the situation of family dynamics when someone finds there is a change in their parent due to a DNA test result is that the sense of belonging to our family keeps us safe, but it will keep others locked out. We need to consider this further.

If our sense of belonging to that original family unit is threatened and we find ourselves in the position of outsider, this brings with it a huge threat, as already considered. But can we belong to two constellations, the old and the new? If we embrace the new, are we feeling we might have lost the original family?

When we have our own family, that becomes the primary unit and the birth family moves to second position. It is known as the 'priority of bonds'. What if there are now two birth families suddenly with half-siblings perhaps? It may feel like difficult territory to negotiate.

We now see a huge increase in blended families, which brings with it challenging loyalties. The pull of 'priority of bonds' can have us feeling like a spinning top.

You may feel that one of your parents has been treated badly or hurt in this situation. They may have been cheated on, or you may even feel concerned for your non-biological parent if they have taken you on as their own. This need to protect in a situation that belongs in the past will be painful and difficult for you to resolve. These are problems that belong to the adults in this situation, and you are the child. Even if you are now an adult, that is not your responsibility; you still hold the child position.

Manné suggests in this situation that making a verbal statement relating to them being big and you small and leaving the adult problems with the adult can be very helpful, again, even if you are now an adult. She even recommends that if doing this within a family constellation session, you kneel on the ground with the parent standing to create this sense of difference and clarity of the position.

As parents get older, they can present as more needy and helpless, but they made the decisions that have affected you many years ago when they were not so, and it is that version of them that you are dealing with. It is important to remember that.

The older, more fragile presenting individual is usually much tougher than you think; they have come through a lifetime of experiences and survived them all. They do not need you to protect them; it is not your job. It was their job to protect you. The ageing of the parent does not ever alter the psychological dynamic. The parents still have a responsibility towards the well-being of the child.

I had an image in my head of my birth family constellation when I first considered it that I will describe for you to help you understand this process.

My father and I are standing close, looking at each other, with my mother in front of us. Just behind him, my grandmother is standing with her arms wrapped around him, but she is looking back over her shoulder. Far back behind us to the left is a dark-haired woman, my aunt, with two small boys, one nine, one six, and a three-year-old little girl, clutching at her. All four are facing away from us with their backs to us; they died before I was born. Just to the right of them is my grandfather, who also died before I was born. He is looking over at us from his position next to them. I had always ascribed my closeness to my father as coming from his early family trauma, which is not a part of this story. I am now wondering if there is some guilt in this due to his secret daughter.

This was the tableaux I had lived with for many years. I now need to adapt it. In a kind of no man's land between the dead and my cluster of survivors stands my half-sister. I see her as a little girl in this. I am looking out from under my father's arm to look at her, this lost-looking little girl, and I am beckoning to her to join us, but to her left, she has another family cluster: her mother, the man she thought of as father and her now half-brother. She looks torn and does not know which way to go. I feel sad and cut off from her and rather caught within this tight group of father and grandmother.

I decided I needed to investigate all this by doing a family constellation session to see how all these dynamics may have affected me and to see how the process works, to see if it can be a useful treatment for people suffering from these DNA revelation events.

Working with my constellation

I will not go into detail here, but I will just walk through the process and show the conclusions so you can appreciate how helpful this kind of therapy can be.

I decided to use the approach with counters to represent the people rather than real participants and to use small objects to represent emotions like guilt, blame, etc, within the family.

When I started laying out the counters, I realised the wider context of my family was not important for this exercise. I set out a trio for myself and my parents, and facing it was my sister with the parents she grew up with, but she is slightly forward from them and looking in our direction.

The counters have faces so you can see where they are facing, and my father is facing in such a way that his gaze is taking in both his daughters. It has been a huge revelation to me that I have realised he contrived to find ways to be close to this other family. It is incredibly obvious to me now, but the light had only just dawned recently that he did share his life with us both. Only, unknowingly to us, that was what he was doing.

This setup in front of me seemed uncomfortable and unresolved. We placed objects on the board to represent my father's guilt, which was huge. There was also an object that represented what I felt I was missing from my family setup, a sense of absence, which was no doubt affecting my sister as well.

Gradually, we shifted positions, bit by bit, to try to find a more comfortable position for the inter-relationships in this complex unification of two families, joined by this breach of family code, infidelity.

As it unfolded, both the mothers seemed to find themselves on the edges of this entanglement, hurt and ignored, as all focus is upon the two children.

I was fascinated at the emotions of empathy I felt for them both, cut adrift from the man they both wanted and from their daughters too, because they perhaps envied that these girls who had their father's attention, either directly or indirectly, would be bound to his girls forever.

I realised that after my father died, he had gifted his guilt towards my mother to me, and I struggled with the huge weight of it; the representation on the board was almost as big as me. I had it virtually on top of me on the board as we moved the counters around. It was a huge awakening to me that I had taken this on, yet perhaps an obvious revelation to an outsider. I promptly moved the representation back to my father. I did not want it anymore; he could keep it. I felt this huge relief as I handed the guilt back. It sat with the adults, as it should. I had not done anything.

I moved my sister closer to me upon the board, and we brought on a new counter for my partner, whom I only just realised was so affected by my role in this constellation. She was there between me and my mother, absorbing and supporting my role and helping support the guilt I had been mistakenly carrying. I suddenly realised how the positions needed to be for me to feel truly comfortable; all four of the adults were now placed together behind me. They had taken their actions in the past, which created this drama in which my sister and I were caught up. They now held the guilt, but then the guilt transmuted into destiny. They had played out their destiny and the future belonged to me/us now, with my partner at my side and my sister nearby. My sister was part of a new family, her own priority family with her boys and partner and also a part of mine, and we needed to leave the past to our parents and all the strain over there with them.

It may be hard to understand how placing some models on a board, asking questions about their roles, their emotions, and moving those positions can lead to enlightenment and release from the past, but I found it hugely liberating. It is something you need to experience to fully appreciate the impact.

I have worked as a therapist for many years now, and this was a new way of looking at families and how to find resolution. I will be looking at ways to incorporate it into my work, having experienced it.

The theory made sense, but the practice of the theory seemed almost esoteric. However, it is an application of common sense and intuition to see how people's roles in families develop, as well as their loyalties. It seems obvious ultimately, but it needs to be experienced, acted out, seen to be fully understood and resolved.

Working as I often do with the unconscious in trance, I think this is another way to tap into that unconscious understanding of what has been happening within a family, bring it into the light and look at what position needs to be taken to find resolution.

I have only given an extremely truncated version of what happened in my session. It took some time and guiding questions about what I felt and how it needed to change, and it would be both intrusive and perhaps too boring to relate to the whole. Also, I was advised not to dwell upon the process but to focus on the outcome – the end positions of the counters. I sat with the end positions and just looked at them for some time. We did not dismantle it straight away, like having a chess board set up to consider your next move, and I have a photograph of it too, to remind me to keep looking forward now instead of looking back over my shoulder at the past. For me this work was the final piece of the jigsaw that gave me peace with my family situation.

Exercise
Making peace with your parents

This exercise is for when you are ready to consider making peace with your parents. So, if you are not ready to think about doing that, leave it for now and keep this exercise tucked away for when you feel able to even try to consider it. This takes time, and only you know how long that time needs to be.

It may help to have a therapist or a close friend to guide you through this process.

You have feelings and responses within you which have been generated by your biological parents; it could be one or both, but we will look at both to be sure we are dealing with all that is there.

So begin by imagining the feelings your mother brings up for you. When you have located that part of you that is responding to your mother, where in your body are you locating those feelings? Is any part of your body responding to this question? When you have located those feelings, give them a colour; it is easier to hold the focus if they have a colour. Hold that colour in the location you have found.

Now imagine that colour flowing from wherever you have found it into the palm of your left hand. Channel all that feeling, that colour, into the palm of your left hand and hold it there. You may find it evolves into a shape in your hand, but it is no problem if it does not; we are just holding that solid mass of colour in the palm of your hand.

Now, I would like you to quickly take your focus away from yourself and look at the room around you, the space around you and note the first letter of three objects that you see in the room around you, thus breaking your focus on this state.

Focus on your biological father now and think of any negative feelings associated there. Find the physical location for those feelings, just as you did with your mother, and give them a colour. Focus on that colour and direct it, channel it into your right hand, see it arrive there, forming a solid shape which may or may not have some significance for you.

Now, look around the room again, see three different objects, and think of the first letter for each.

Bring an image of your mother to your mind and ask the question, 'What good were you trying to do for me, Mother, by acting as you did?' The act and the result may feel very different to the outcome you experienced, but what was your mother trying to do, even if she failed to do so, in your eyes? Think about her intentions.

Bring an image of your father to your mind and ask the question, 'What good were you trying to do for me, Father, by acting as you did?' The act and the result may feel very different to the outcome you experienced, but what was your father trying to do, even if he failed to do so, in your eyes? Think about his intentions.

Thank these representations of your parents for being there to help you understand what was happening when you feel you have found an answer. If nothing comes up, then perhaps the time is not yet right for you to follow this process.

Tell both those parts, the mother and the father, to appreciate the role they played in attempting to do this for you.

To feel integrated and whole, bring your two hands together slowly to combine the two parts and integrate them. As you do this, you feel more whole, united, no longer divided. This new combined part can reside somewhere within you, and it has its own new and positive colour. I wonder what it is?

Now, see a timeline that represents your life, perhaps a translucent pathway of light. It stretches far into the future and back into the past. Take these new feelings you have represented by the new colour, and float back along the line to your birth and then bring this feeling of wholeness and integration along the line to today. Take your time working through all your life to this point now. You can then do a mini jump into the future, a year from now and see how things have changed for you. Observe yourself looking happier, calmer, more at peace with yourself. That's right. Now, bring that feeling back into the present you. You feel much better now. More at peace.

If any aspect of this process has been difficult for you, leave it for a few months and come back to it. Notice the changes the second time you experience it.

Exercise
Younger and older self, visualisation

I would like you to imagine that you are sitting on the bank of a river, for now, just passing time, watching the water flowing past, you might hear some birdsong, you can hear the sound of the rushing water, it is a warm summer day, you feel the warmth of the sun upon your skin, but it is not too hot, there is a gentle breeze, and you may feel it ruffling your hair or your clothing.

You can see the sunlight glinting off the surface of water, there are pebbles visible beneath the shallow water at the edge of the river, the water is crystal clear, really focus in and hear the bubbling sound as the water rushes past you on its journey, be present in this moment by the water, your life is rather like this flowing water, sometimes it rushes so fast there seems hardly any time to focus on taking things in to make a decision to know how you feel and at other times when perhaps you are waiting for something to happen it feels so very slow, almost stagnant.

You visit different places on that journey, you see all sorts of people, form relationships. Some stay the same, and some change; some need to be reevaluated, and you learn from those experiences, which are ever-changing with the flow of your life. It is important to recognize that nothing is static. It is ever-evolving, ever-changing like the flow of that river.

I would like you to imagine now there is a boat coming along the river towards you from the left-hand side, and on that boat is your younger self, perhaps late teens or maybe early twenties. This younger self has not experienced the new knowledge that you have to process now; this younger you is unaware of what lies ahead for them, but they have a message for you, something that can help you at this point in your life, as you deal with this new information, you perhaps not yet had some of the experiences that limit you now, nothing to do with the struggles of this moment,

What is their advice for you now.....how important is this new knowledge for your life experience? Take some time to listen to them, do not dismiss the wisdom that your younger self can bring you that has perhaps been lost in the twists and turns of your life like the twists and turns of the flow of the river....they step off their boat onto the river bank and they share with you.....listen to the wisdom....it is not only age that brings knowledge and perspective, youth brings an enthusiasm and a dynamism that we sometimes lose sight of as we get older.

Argue for your limitations and you will indeed be limited....use the resilience of your younger self to help you right now......take some time to absorb what this younger you has to give you.............listen and learn, there is more here than you can realise if you get stuck with how you feel right now.

When you are ready and only when you are ready, I would like you to say goodbye and give thanks to your younger self for their support, but before they have a chance to board their boat, another boat comes into view....this time from the right- hand side of the river. On this boat is a much older you....older than you are now....this older you has a message too....a message for your life now.

They have passed through your current moment, they have come to terms with this, found perspective, seen what can come from it, has learned to live with it, they are so much further ahead dealing with this ....they have lived through it and so much more...so I wonder what they have to say to you...what advice they can give you to help you move on your journey down the river...moving smoothly...not too fast...not too slow..... what will they tell you.....? So allow them to get off their boat and join you on the river bank and take some time, time with them to absorb their wisdom......

How did they get through this? How did they deal with the people around them whom they possibly blamed for the secret, how did they talk about this to others, what did they do and how can they help you? They know what to do, so listen....open your mind and listen...

When you have had enough time with this older you, allow both of your visitors to greet each other. It's interesting for you to watch them, the past and the future you, a harmony of past, present and future that makes up your journey.

Take a moment to integrate this new learning, whatever it has brought to you.

Then the time comes for the past and future you to depart, leaving with you their wisdom. First, the past you boards their boat and begins to drift away towards the left-hand side of the river, then the future you takes their leave and heads down the right-hand side of the river, moving away from you, but their messages remain with you, comforting you, take some time now to feel the calm of this knowledge to move through you, feel it and know it now.....

It may be that all they can share with you takes some time to filter through, so if nothing much comes through the first time you do this, give it time. Your mind will find what it needs at the right time and now open your eyes and come back into the room.

Write down anything from this experience that will help you now; any feelings, revelations from the past or your projected future. You may wish to do it a couple of times to really get the full benefit of the exercise.

Chapter fifteen

CONCLUSION

As I drew near to the end of writing this book, the Christmas season was approaching. As I sat scrolling through the news on my phone over breakfast, I saw an article on all the Christmas TV ads from the usual big players. I clicked on the John Lewis advertisement with little interest, and by the end of it, I was crying, really sobbing. Yet this year's ad had been written off as missing the usual emotional quotient, but not for me.

It was a story of two sisters meeting at John Lewis to go shopping and the ad was full of flashbacks to the sisters' shared past. It showed me a snapshot of what my sister and I had been denied, and it hurt. I sent the clip through to my sister, saying, 'This made me cry', and she quickly replied that it had done the same to her too. Nobody else I knew seemed to be moved by the ad, just us. It did not leave others basking in sisterly sentimentality, but when you have missed so many shared experiences, it really hurts.

I had not, at this point, written the integration piece for the book; it had been developing in my mind, and I knew I had to stop procrastinating and write, so it gradually took shape. It was so therapeutic to do, and

I shed some more tears along the way. It could have become too indulgent; I could have delved deep but decided to keep it short to not lose myself in it, which really helped. We will never know whether our lives would have been better or worse if our story had been out in the open. There are so many alternative possibilities as to how it could have played out, and my version is undoubtedly the most positive. It could have been much worse for all of us. The fact is that we have to learn to live with what is and that we will never know what could have been.

That is the difficulty in our story: so much not knowing. You may share this in your story, or you may have more answers than we do. We are surrounded by uncertainty, and as humans, we find this very uncomfortable. Accepting and tolerating uncertainty is part of the journey.

Coming to terms with the kind of changes DNA revelations can bring is a slow process. I still have my moments of denial, as so much of my life was a different story. It is a default setting to dive back into the comfort of it. I have been through a therapeutic journey of my own using some of the techniques I describe in the book and by writing the book. I can only hope that they will help others, too, as there seems so little out there to help the growing numbers in this position.

I have shared some of our story to help others feel perhaps more understood and less alone with the seismic shift in their life story. It is not easy to process even when you have a vast psychological toolkit to dip into. You still have to do the work of reconciliation with the past and with yourself.

I have found it interesting that stories in books and films about families discovering paternity events that I might have encountered before when revisited cut me so deeply. There are triggers everywhere you turn these days; it is a common story. Despite the commonality, it causes huge pain and struggle for all involved. It is used as a foil for entertainment, but it is not pure entertainment for me; it is a mirror to look in and try to recognise the new reflection that you see.

Everyone is affected in the family story: parents, siblings, cousins, aunts, and children; the impact ripples out even into family friends.

Bereavement is generally expected by the therapy community to take about two years to work through the worst of the emotional turmoil, and I have already said this identity change is a bereavement of a kind, a bereavement of the life you thought you had and the old view of the self, whatever your role in the story.

It has been just over two years for me now, and it is much, much easier, and I think it is for my sister, too, but there is no set time. It is your time to process the changes in your story. It will be easier if you do not hide from it but try to work with it and try ultimately to find the good in it. There is growth to be found and self-awareness, and if you are lucky, new family connections. But I say again, your past was true, too; you lived through it, and no one can steal it from you.

ACKNOWLEDGEMENTS

I would like to thank my sister for being everything I could have wanted in a sister and for supporting me in writing this book that exposes our family to the spotlight yet again. I was just finishing writing *The Trauma Effect* when we first met, which plunged her straight into coming to terms with a family tragedy, though reading about it in a book. I have not named her at any point as I feel she must oversee her own destiny and with whom she decides to share her part of this story. Each time we meet, I am still astounded by how strong our kinship feels and how much we have in common, which makes it an even greater blessing.

I can only tell this story from my perspective, though I hope showing empathy for hers.

My partner Evelyn Meyer has accompanied me on yet another journey of discovery into my family, which has brought with it many ups and, at first, a few downs. She has listened patiently to stories of old memories, engaging with a cast of characters and scenes that lie way behind us in the past.

Jane German, my first cousin and fellow only child growing up, has always been the sister I did not think I had. She has been there through thick and thin, and this latest experience has been no exception. It was she who understood my careering emotions when all this unfolded, as she was also very close to her own father and, as I said, an only child too. We had been brought up like sisters with two sets of parents, so this change in the family dynamics rocked her world too. Having a sister now does not change our life story together any more than my sister's brother would find himself relegated to a different position. My sister and I must be seen as additions to our existing family constellations and no doubt it causes some ripples, but the foundations remain the same. I thank Jane for all the listening she has done and for still being there.

Lena Sefrin was the friend who was there on the fateful day that I found out about my sister. She shared her story, showing me happy photos of her and her new sister on her phone. At that point, I could not imagine being in that place of peace, but she gave me an example to follow and truly shared and understood the journey I was embarking upon.

My cousin Isobel Williams brought thoughtful and insightful questioning of my feelings, which helped me greatly in the first days of this revelation, and she patiently waited for the light to dawn as she helped me towards integration.

My sister-in-law, Sigrid Malike, guided me with such skill and empathy through my family constellation experience and made a huge contribution to my current peace of mind, which has allowed me to leave all the guilt and shame with the previous generation. I am determined we will not carry it for them anymore.

I would like to thank my patient readers, Maureen Williams, my long-term mentor, and Julie Adams, whose painstaking work going through the text certainly made this a better book. Also, thanks must go to Michelle Emerson, my editor, proofreader and designer. It is such a relief to find a competent proofreader at last.

It never ceases to amaze me how a book starts out as an idea, often very fragmented, and ends up eventually complete and you know when to put the final full stop, and I am there now.

REFERENCES

Chapter two – The test

Copeland, L. (2020) *The Lost Family, How DNA Testing Is Upending Who We Are.* Abrams Press page 4, ibid 79, ibid 271

Chapter six – Identity

Greenfield, S. (2011) *You and Me: The Neuroscience of Identity.* Notting Hill Editions Ltd. page 2, ibid 21

Nevslin, I. (2019) *The Impact of Identity.* Amazon. page 17

Greenfield, S. (2011) *You and Me: The Neuroscience of Identity.* Notting Hill Editions Ltd. page 1, ibid 81, ibid 16

Maslow, A.H. (2022) *A Theory of Human Motivation.* Wilder Publications. pages 33-34

Nevslin, I. (2019) *The Impact of Identity.* Amazon. page 57-58

Castells, M. (2014) 'The impact of internet on society, a global perspective.' MIT Technology Review

Greenfield, S. (2011) *You and Me: The Neuroscience of Identity.* Notting Hill Editions Ltd. page 57

Nevslin, I. (2019) *The Impact of Identity.* Amazon. page 69, ibid 82, ibid 94

Greenfield, S. (2011) *You and Me: The Neuroscience of Identity.* Notting Hill Editions Ltd. page 96, ibid 59

Balick, A. Dr. (2013) *The Psychodynamics of Social Networking.* Routledge. page 42, Ibid 153, ibid 80

Brown, B. (2012) *Daring Greatly.* Penguin Random House. pages 18-21

Fearon, J. D. (1999) 'What is Identity (As We Now Use The Word)?' Dept of Political Science Stanford University. page 9

Chapter seven – Secrets and lies

Weir, K. (September 2020) 'Exposing The Hidden World of Secrets.' American Psychological Association. Vol 51 no 6

Bok, S. (2011) *Secrets: On the Ethics of Concealment and Revelation.* Knopf Doubleday Publishing Group. page 25

Bok, S. (1978) *Lying Moral Choice in Public and Private Life.* Quartet Books, pages 21-24, ibid 94

Copeland, L. (2020) *The Lost Family, How DNA Testing Is Upending Who We Are.* Abrams Press. page 210, ibid 218-219

Schwab, G. (2010) *Haunting Legacies, Violent Histories and Transgenerational Trauma.* Columbia University Press

Kubler-Ross, E. and Kessler, D. (2014) *On Grief and Grieving.* Simon and Schuster UK. pages 85-86

Chapter nine – Shame

Kämmerer, A. (2019) *The Scientific Underpinnings of the Impact of Shame.* Scientific American

Brown, B. (2012) *Daring Greatly.* Penguin Random House. pages 61-67, ibid 76

Preiss Torten, I. (2012) *Family Constellations Revealed: Hellinger's Family and other Constellations Revealed (The Systemic View).* Independently Published. page 12

Office of National Statistics Births in England and Wales 2022

'Sources of Family Breakdown in the UK' Harry Benson Marriage Foundation July 2023 page 1

Chapter ten – Grief and loss

Kubler-Ross, E. and Kessler, D. (2014) *On Grief and Grieving.* Simon and Schuster UK. page 8, ibid 11-14

Nevslin, I. (2019) *The Impact of Identity.* Amazon. page 30, ibid 35

Chapter eleven – Anger

Deffenbacher, J. L. PhD and McKay, M. PhD. (2000) *Overcoming Situational and Generational Anger* New Harbinger Publications. pages 1-8

Williams, R. (2017 Nov 7; 8:1950) *Anger as a Basic Emotion and Its Role in Personality Building and Pathological Growth: The Neuroscientific, Developmental and Clinical Perspectives.* Frontiers in Psychology

Battino, R. MS. *Metaphoria: Metaphor and Guided Imagery for Psychotherapy and Healing.* Crown House Publishing. pages 1-7

Chapter eleven – Belonging

Brown, B. (2012) *Daring Greatly.* Penguin Random House. page 145

Springtide Research Institute www.springtideresearch.org

Allen, K-A. et al. (2022) *The Need to Belong: A Deep Dive into the Origins, Implications, and Future of a Foundational Construct.* Educational Psychological Review 34 (2) 1133-1136

Brown, B. (2012) *Daring Greatly.* Penguin Random House. page 232

Chapter twelve – Family constellation therapy

Gilbert, R. M. MD. (2004) *The Eight Concepts of Bowen Theory.* Leading Systems Press. pages 2-6, ibid 78, ibid 35

Manné, J. (2005) *Family Constellations A Practical Guide to Uncovering the Origins of Family Conflict.* Atlantic Books. pages 3-7, ibid 52

www.ingramcontent.com/pod-product-compliance
Ingram Content Group UK Ltd.
Pitfield, Milton Keynes, MK11 3LW, UK
UKHW011431060925
462636UK00002B/127